BULBS

Richard Rosenfeld

**LONDON, NEW YORK,
MUNICH, MELBOURNE, DELHI**

Series Editor Helen Fewster
Series Art Editor Alison Donovan
Designer Rachael Smith
Editor Victoria Willan
Managing Editor Anna Kruger
Managing Art Editor Lee Griffiths
Consultant Louise Abbott
DTP Designer Louise Waller
Media Resources Lucy Claxton
Picture Research Samantha Nunn
Index Michèle Clarke
Production Controller Mandy Inness
US Editor Christine Heilman
US Senior Editor Jill Hamilton
US Editorial Assistant John Searcy

First American Edition, 2004

Published in the United States by
DK Publishing, Inc.
375 Hudson Street
New York, New York 10014

04 05 06 07 08 10 9 8 7 6 5 4 3 2 1

A Cataloging-in-Publication record for this book
is available from the Library of Congress.

ISBN 0-7566-0356-0

Color reproduction by Colourscan, Singapore
Printed and bound in Italy by Printer Trento

Discover more at
www.dk.com

Gardening with bulbs

Bulbs are astonishing, power-packed structures. Each one stores the energy that it needs to grow and flower as soon as the right conditions occur. All you need to do is put them in a hole in the ground, provide the kind of conditions they would get in the wild, and let them get on with it, sometimes with a prayer and a bit of pampering.

Bulbs can be grown all around the garden in a variety of situations, in pots, beds, and borders, as well as in open lawns and the light shade under trees where the spreaders can quickly create large clumps. Bulbs from countries with hot, dry, baking summers are best grown in rockeries or in soil with excellent drainage in front of sunny walls, where they can be tricked into thinking they are somewhere like South Africa. And if you're worried about spearing through them with a garden fork while giving the garden a makeover, use discreet positional markers or grow the bulbs where you rarely do any digging—for example, around the base of shrubs.

One final tip—get mail-order catalogs from specialist suppliers. They invariably have the widest, most exciting, up-to-date range of bulbs.

◀ **Grape hyacinths** are excellent in cottage gardens, where they create a superb spread of bright blue in spring.

▶ **The extraordinary flowers** of the crown imperial fritillary add an exotic touch.

Bluebells are ideal for planting in bold groups in cool, shady parts of the garden. Grow them at the base of trees to create a colorful woodland look.

The spring garden

The spring bulbs kick off with the daffodils. Besides the yellow and white kind, some have red, orange, or pink centers, and then there are the miniature tazettas. Grow them in pots indoors and their scent will fill a room. Tiny anemones and the delicate flowers of the dog's-tooth violet add a gentle woodland touch, and tulips can be used in strong, formal plans.

The tulips include some of the liveliest, richest colors. Yes, they are slightly work-intensive because most have to be dug up and kept dry over summer, but their petals include bright, brash reds, near-blacks, purples, lipstick pinks, and butter yellows. Before buying them, stand in different garden positions and clarify exactly what colors you need, and where; the foreground tulips will have to work with those behind, and even with those in the distance, because all the colors will stand out sharply next spring. Get the layout right now, at the planning stage. You can't rearrange the bulbs when they are flowering.

Summer bulbs

Bulbs also provide good strong shapes and surprise value. The drumstick alliums with their tight-packed ball of flowers, ranging from the size of a golf ball to that of a melon, can be used to flank paths, encircle island beds, and rise up beneath laburnum trees whose yellow flowers hang down in thickets.

Lilies can be equally astonishing, and many are amazingly scented. The taller ones can thrust up powerful stems to a height of 6ft (2m), while the flowers come in a range of

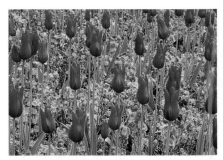

Tulips can be used in a wide range of color combinations, including this upbeat orange plan.

Pinkish purple fritillaries make an excellent, gentle spring display for a patio container.

End-of-season highs

Bulbs are also good at adding rich colors through the second half of summer, into autumn, long after the spring hullabaloo.

shapes from large, open trumpets to the small, speckled blooms that look like huge butterflies hovering above the border.

The giant lily (*Cardiocrinum giganteum*) also has plenty of impact. Unlike most lilies, it thrives in cool, moist parts of the garden where it puts out strongly perfumed flowers. It is a superb Himalayan bulb for borders locked in shade.

Many dahlias have enormous heads in strong colors and interesting, spiky shapes, but you can also get the smaller-flowering kinds, like 'Glorie van Heemstede', which has a clear yellow face. Dahlias add plenty of zip, just like the American cannas, which have surprisingly small, often brightly colored flowers, while the best (like 'Striata') add fun, eye-catching leaves.

Tomato red crocosmias are cleverly quieted down by the use of purple verbena.

They are just a fraction of the bulbs available. Bulbs add extra layers of interest at every height and at every level, like the tiny, 5in- (13cm-) high *Cyclamen hederifolium*. Get close and you'll see the leaves have patterned, silvery speckles—as beautiful a sight as any, especially in the middle of autumn, in the sunlight between the trees.

White summer snowflakes make a bright choice for a wild or cottage garden display, livening up shady areas around trees and shrubs.

Buying and planting bulbs

BUY BULBS THE MOMENT they are available in garden centers, but be wary of those sold in stores where they might deteriorate or start to sprout too early due to hot, bright conditions. Generally, plant them as soon as possible, but note that tulips should not go in the ground until midautumn in case they shoot up and get caught by a frost.

Bulbs

The word *bulb* is an all-embracing term covering bulbs, tubers, and corms. They are all highly condensed storage organs that wait until the surface conditions are right before shooting up into a mature plant. Flowering is followed by a dormant spell, when the surface conditions are inappropriate for growth. If you slice a typical bulb vertically in half, you will generally find a protective tunic outside, tightly packed scales underneath for storing food, then the embryo stem, the future leaves and flowers packed tightly inside, and, at the bottom, a plate where the roots grow. When choosing true bulbs, select large, firm, healthy ones; reject any that "give" and those with cuts, bruises, or mold.

Hyacinth

Tulip

Single-nosed daffodil

Twin-nosed daffodil

Tubers, corms, and rhizomes

These are slightly different kinds of storage organs, the difference being that tubers are actually swollen stems or roots, corms are a swollen piece of last year's stem, and rhizomes are swollen, modified stems. These botanical terms are rarely used in this book. They are all variants on the same theme, and it's not always easy to tell one from another; erythronium bulbs are often confused with other organs.

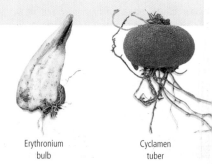

Erythronium bulb

Cyclamen tuber

Preparing the site

Good drainage is frequently important because most bulbs like to be on the dry side when dormant. That means forking up the soil and, if necessary, adding sand and grit.

Blood, fish, and bone

Bone meal

Feeding plants

Fork concentrated organic fertilizers, such as bone meal or blood, fish, and bone, which release their nutrients slowly, well into the soil; do not leave on the surface.

Planting bulbs with leaves on

Some bulbs—for example, snowdrops (*Galanthus*)—need to be planted just after flowering when they are still carrying their leaves, a stage called "in the green."

Planting in the green

Make sure the bulbs are planted so that the soil level is flush with the junction of the leaves and the sheath at the top of the bulb.

Planting depths

The planting hole should usually be twice the depth of the solid chunk of the bulb on heavy ground, and three times the depth of the bulb where the soil is lighter and more free-draining. (Tulips, however, should be planted at four times their own depth.) Separate bulbs by two to three times their own width.

Planting in layers

Get a succession of flowers by planting bulbs in two layers in a container. The lower level will flower slightly later.

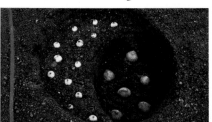

Planting small bulbs in grass

When planting large numbers of small bulbs in a lawn, it's impossible to make hundreds of individual holes. You need to create flaps in the grass and arrange the bulbs at irregular intervals—about 1in (2.5cm) apart—so that they do not pop up in strict, military rows.

Note that the leaves of all bulbs (especially those in lawns) must be allowed to die down naturally because they help store energy for next year's display. Allow six weeks after flowering for daffodils, and four for crocuses. Do not prematurely mow them off.

1 Create a flap
Use a spade to create an *H* shape in the grass. Make sure that it slices down cleanly through the sod into the soil below. Then carefully peel back the flaps to reveal the soil.

2 Planting the bulbs
Fork up the soil to a depth of 3in (7cm). If it is hard and compact, add a scattering of bone meal and then set out the bulbs, gently pressing them into the ground.

3 Roll back and firm
Finally, roll back the sod and cover the bulbs, but take care not to damage their growing points while doing so. Firm the grass into position and avoid walking on it.

Forcing prepared bulbs

It is possible to make some bulbs flower early indoors, especially during winter. They are known as "forced bulbs" and have been specially prepared by keeping them in the dark to get unnaturally quick results. Good candidates include hyacinths and small, sweetly scented daffodils.

Forcing hyacinths
Plant three bulbs in a container of moist bulb potting mix, leaving their tips to poke through the surface. Keep them in a cool, dark place. When yellowish buds appear, move to a cool, bright position for flowering.

Routine care

BULBS THRIVE IN THE WILD without any help, and provided they are given the right garden conditions, you can usually leave them alone. But some definitely benefit from a helping hand. Besides weeding to eradicate aggressive competitors, that usually means staking, feeding, mulching, deadheading, and dividing the bulbs when clumps become congested.

Supporting tall bulbs

Some flowering bulbs such as lilies, gladiolus, dahlias, and camassias need a strong support to keep them from flopping over and to allow them to be seen clearly. Either put the canes near the bulbs at planting time when you know where they are buried, or wait until the stems start shooting up.

Staking a group of lilies
Use soft garden twine to make a figure-eight loop when securing stems.

Staking a gladiolus
Tie in the stems when 6in (15cm) high, and later just below flower buds.

Feeding

Give bulbs liquid tomato fertilizer after flowering, but while still in leaf, to inject extra energy for next year's display. When the foliage yellows, stop watering because the bulbs are about to become dormant.

Liquid feeding
Use half-strength fertilizer that is high in potash. Water in the early morning or evening to avoid scorching the leaves.

Winter mulching

Spreading extra layers of organic material on the soil surface (mulching) helps to keep out the cold over winter. The mulch acts like a blanket, protecting more tender bulbs from diving temperatures, and improves the soil.

Applying a mulch
Winter is the best time to mulch, since the plants are dormant. If you mulch at other times, make sure the soil beneath is moist.

Deadheading and cutting down

The way to encourage bulbs to flower well in future displays is to cut off fading blooms promptly. This stops plants from putting their energy into making seeds and self-propagating, and diverts them into producing more flowers. If it is not in the bulb's genetic code to flower again now, deadheading will help it to save energy for the following year's display.

However, some bulbs, like the drumstick alliums, produce quite startling seedheads that are worth leaving to add extra shapes in borders. You can also snip them off for use in flower arrangements.

Removing seedheads
Cut the dead flower stems (here alliums) down to ground level using pruners.

Cutting down after flowering
As well as removing fading flowers, also cut off the leaves when they start to lose their color. If they are removed any sooner, the bulbs will not perform well in future years.

Dividing bulbs

Left to their own devices, bulbs often form congested clumps, all tightly packed together, and flowering starts to decline significantly. When this happens, carefully fork up the entire clump in the dormant season, and tease apart the sections. Each section can then be replanted around the garden at the same depth as before. If the poorly performing clump is not congested, then try moving it to another, more appropriate site.

1 Dig up the clump
When the leaves start fading, the bulbs are becoming dormant; lever them out of the ground with a fork.

2 Pry the clump apart
Carefully divide it into smaller sections, but if it is really stuck together, try loosening it with water.

3 Check the bulbs
Take this opportunity to inspect the bulbs closely, and discard any that might be damaged or unhealthy.

Lifting and storing bulbs

MANY BULBS COME FROM REGIONS where they get a baking hot summer. The last thing they need is to keep getting drenched in downpours, or spend days in cold, wet soil.

Others will not survive bad winters. This is why some bulbs need to be dug up after their leaves have faded, to be stored in cool, dry conditions while they are dormant.

1 Lifting
Remove the bulbs (here tulips) when the leaves have faded, taking great care not to spear them with a fork. Put them in labeled containers.

2 Cleaning
Gently remove the soil and pull away any loose tissue covering the bulb. Then cut off the base of the stem. Discard any damaged or diseased bulbs.

3 Treating
Spread the bulbs out on a wire rack and allow them to dry overnight. The following day, lightly dust each bulb with a fungicide to help prevent them from rotting.

4 Storage
Store the bulbs in clearly labeled paper bags or trays. Keep them in a cool, dry place and check them regularly, promptly removing any bulbs that show signs of disease.

A-Z of Bulbs

A

Albuca humilis

EACH WHITE FLOWER of *Albuca humilis* (there are usually from one to three) has highly distinct inner and outer petals. The green-striped outer ones point outward like propellers, and the yellow-tipped inner ones are so close together that they almost look like a tube. Being tender, it's best grown in a pot, filled with a loam-based potting mix and added horticultural sand, in a cool greenhouse. Give it water and liquid fertilizer while it's growing, then dry it off as it becomes dormant. *A. humilis* tends to be grown by specialists, but beginners might be able to grow it outside in mild areas in a sheltered site. A cloche in winter gives added protection.

OTHER VARIETY *A. nelsonii* (white flowers with a green, or sometimes red, central stripe).

PLANT PROFILE
HEIGHT 2–4in (5–10cm)
SPREAD 2–3in (5–8cm)
SITE Full sun
SOIL Light, free-draining
HARDINESS Z11–12 H12–10
FLOWERING Late spring and early summer

Allium cernuum Wild onion

WILD ONION'S SPRAYS OF TINY, pink, nodding blooms make good cut flowers, and appear on stiff stems, adding a quietly understated touch to the front of borders, or gravel or rock gardens. Widely found growing across North America, from the far north down to Mexico, *Allium cernuum* requires good sun and drainage. The undemanding bulbs soon multiply, forming attractive clumps that are good at withstanding heavy midsummer downpours.

OTHER VARIETY *A. carinatum* (bell-shaped, purple flowers).

PLANT PROFILE
HEIGHT 12–24in (30–60cm)
SPREAD 2in (5cm)
SITE Full sun
SOIL Fertile, free-draining
HARDINESS Z3–9 H9–5
FLOWERING Summer

A | *Allium cristophii* Stars of Persia

THIS TERRIFIC ALLIUM'S ENORMOUS round flowerhead (it measures about 8in/20cm wide) consists of dozens of tiny, star-shaped flowers, and sits on top of a long, sturdy stem. *Allium cristophii* is dramatically striking partly because its leaves wither before the flowers have fully opened, and therefore don't distract from the blooms. The seedheads make a lively focal point in dried flower arrangements. The best growing conditions are wall-to-wall sun and good drainage; feeding is rarely required. If you want an allium with an even larger flowerhead, go for the pale purple *A. schubertii*, which is up to 12in (30cm) wide.

OTHER VARIETY *A*. 'Globemaster' (deep violet flowers).

PLANT PROFILE

HEIGHT 12–24in (30–60cm)

SPREAD 6–8in (15–20cm)

SITE Full sun

SOIL Average, free-draining

HARDINESS Z3–9 H9–5

FLOWERING Early summer

Allium cyathophorum var. *farreri* Onion

A

AN EASILY GROWN, VERY SMALL Chinese onion, *Allium cyathophorum* var. *farreri* has clusters of tiny flowers, totaling up to 30, that are bell-shaped and deep violet purple. The bulbs quickly form clumps, but once you have enough plants, snip off the flowers as they fade to stop them from scattering their seed and multiplying even more. Bright sun is best, but plants will adapt to shady conditions, where they are equally prolific. Grow them toward the front of borders, or in rock and gravel gardens (where the roots need a good depth of soil). Summer watering ensures that the ground doesn't bake dry for too long.

OTHER VARIETY *A. flavum* (bell-shaped, bright yellow flowers).

PLANT PROFILE
HEIGHT 6–12in (15–30cm)
SPREAD 2in (5cm)
SITE Full sun
SOIL Fertile, free-draining, rich in organic matter
HARDINESS Z4–9 H9–1
FLOWERING Summer

A | *Allium fistulosum* Welsh onion

PLANT PROFILE

ACTUALLY A VEGETABLE, *Allium fistulosum* can also be grown for its attractive, yellow-white flowers, which appear on top of the upright, bright green stems. It's best planted in bold groups next to strong reds or blues. Sow the seeds where the plants are to grow in spring, (or in August to flower the following year) in rows about 7in (18cm) apart; when they come up, pull some out, leaving the rest 6in (15cm) apart. Leave to flower every year or use the stems, which do not die back in mild winters, in salads and soups.

HEIGHT To 2ft (60cm)

SPREAD To 9in (23cm)

SITE Full sun

SOIL Fertile, free-draining

HARDINESS Z4–9

FLOWERING Early to midsummer

Allium hollandicum 'Purple Sensation' Onion

A

THIS IS AN INCREDIBLY USEFUL and popular plant because of its round, tennis ball–like flowerheads, consisting of hundreds of tiny, strong purple flowers packed together on top of a long, sturdy stem. The heads are a modest 3in (8cm) wide, and are not outrageously large like those of *Allium schubertii*. *A. hollandicum* 'Purple Sensation' can easily be positioned in borders, but because one by itself is not enough, plant the bulbs in groups or in intermittent rows to draw the eye along. It looks superb under the dangling yellow flowers of *Laburnum* x *watereri* 'Vossii'. Provide wall-to-wall sun and good drainage; feeding is rarely required.

OTHER VARIETY *A. giganteum* (star-shaped, lilac-pink flowers).

PLANT PROFILE	
HEIGHT To 3ft (1m)	
SPREAD 3in (8cm)	
SITE Full sun	
SOIL Fertile, moist but free-draining	
HARDINESS Z4–9 H12–1	
FLOWERING Late spring, early summer	

A | *Allium karataviense* Turkestan onion

ONE OF THE SMALLEST ONIONS—it looks dwarfed against the enormous 6ft- (2m-) high *Allium giganteum*—*A. karataviense* has pairs of broad, almost horizontal, grayish purple-green leaves with a red margin. The red tends to fade as the large round buds (*see inset*) open, producing pale pink flowers. Grow it away from other plants where it can be seen more easily, in a free-draining, sunny, gravel garden, or try it with other small-leaved plants including marjoram (*Origanum* 'Kent Beauty'). Because one by itself looks very odd, grow it in small groups—for example, edging a gravel path.

PLANT PROFILE	
HEIGHT 4–10in (10–25cm)	
SPREAD 4–10in (10–25cm)	
SITE Full sun	
SOIL Free-draining	
HARDINESS Z3–9 H9–5	
FLOWERING Late spring	

Allium moly Golden garlic

A

IF YOU NEED A THOROUGHLY RELIABLE, golden yellow–flowering onion, *Allium moly* is one of the best of to go for. It is perfectly happy in full sun or dappled shade, and can be grown around deciduous shrubs—where it quickly multiplies, covering the bare soil—or at the front of a border. If too many plants start appearing and it gets too prolific, just fork the ones you don't want out of the ground. *A. moly* can also be grown at the sunny edge of a woodland garden, where it can form impressive, spreading clumps.

OTHER VARIETY *A. moly* 'Jeannine' (taller, with larger flowerheads).

PLANT PROFILE
HEIGHT 6–10in (15–25cm)
SPREAD 2in (5cm)
SITE Full sun or dappled shade
SOIL Fertile, free-draining
HARDINESS Z3–9 H9–1
FLOWERING Early summer

A | *Allium neapolitanum* Daffodil garlic

A RAMPANT ONION FOR WARM, sheltered gardens, *Allium neapolitanum* produces a mass of green leaves, up to 14in (35cm) long, topped by wiry stems with tiny, white, star-shaped flowers that are good for cutting. *A. neapolitanum* adds a free and easy charm, and often flowers in late spring rather than early summer, but it needs a position where it can be clearly seen—for example, at the front of a border, or in a rock or gravel garden. After flowering, the bulbs like to bake over summer while dormant.

OTHER VARIETY *A. cupanii* (pink-white with a darker central vein).

PLANT PROFILE

HEIGHT	8–16in (20–40cm)
SPREAD	2in (5cm)
SITE	Full sun
SOIL	Fertile, free-draining
HARDINESS	Z7–9 H9–7
FLOWERING	Early summer

Allium schoenoprasum Chives

 A

BRIGHTLY COLORED, with fresh green leaves and small purple flowers, chives can be used in herb gardens, pots, or windowboxes. The bright green, hollow leaves, up to 14in (35cm) long, are the edible part. Sprinkle them on salads, soups, or baked potatoes, and use them in egg dishes. If a recipe calls for a large amount of chives, cut them back hard with a pair of scissors, leaving 1in (2.5cm) of growth in summer, and tasty new shoots will soon appear. Plant chives in rich soil if possible, although they will tolerate poorer ground, and make sure that new plants are well watered in summer.

PLANT PROFILE
HEIGHT 5–10in (12–25cm)
SPREAD 2–4in (5–10cm)
SITE Full sun
SOIL Fertile, moist but free-draining
HARDINESS Z5–11 H9–1
FLOWERING Summer

A | *Allium unifolium* One-leafed onion

DESPITE ITS COMMON NAME, *Allium unifolium* will sometimes grow multiple leaves, which are gray-green and appear down at ground level. The foliage withers before the relatively large, bell-shaped, sugary purple-pink flowers appear in a cluster at the end of spring. The North American *A. unifolium* is best grown in large-scale rock gardens, because it's a bit too tall for the small, miniature kind. It is not totally hardy, and requires a sunny, sheltered position.

OTHER VARIETY *A. neapolitanum* (*see page 24*).

PLANT PROFILE	
HEIGHT	12in (30cm)
SPREAD	2in (5cm)
SITE	Full sun
SOIL	Fertile, free-draining
HARDINESS	Z4–9 H9–1
FLOWERING	Spring

x *Amarcrinum memoria-corsii*

A

WITH ITS SMALL, SCENTED, trumpet-shaped flowers, which are up to 4in (10cm) long and emerge in clusters of about ten, x *Amarcrinum memoria-corsii* deserves to be much more popular. The 24in- (60cm-) long leaves hang on all year in mild, sheltered gardens. An easy plant to grow if you can provide average, free-draining soil in a sunny, frost-free site—for example, at the base of a sheltering wall—it looks good next to the taller, 5ft- (1.5m-) high *Crinum* x *powellii* (*see page 64*), which likes similar conditions. Plant the bulb with its tip just below soil level, and look out for slugs when new growth starts.

PLANT PROFILE	
HEIGHT 3ft (1m)	
SPREAD 24in (60cm)	
SITE Full sun	
SOIL Average, free-draining	
HARDINESS Z13–15 H12–9	
FLOWERING Late summer	

A

x *Amarygia parkeri* 'Alba'

THIS PRETTY AND HIGHLY USEFUL BULB can be tricky to find in catalogs and does not often get a mention in gardening books, but is well worth tracking down. Its trumpet-shaped, amaryllis-like flowers emerge in clusters of up to 12, and are 2½–4in (6–10cm) long. The leaves are like long, green straps, up to 18in (45cm) long, and only appear after flowering. Plant x *Amarygia parkeri* 'Alba' with the nose of the bulb just above the soil, which should be rich in organic matter, sandy, and free-draining. Make sure the bulbs are planted in a sunny, sheltered, frost-free site—for example, at the foot of a wall.

PLANT PROFILE	
HEIGHT 3ft (1m)	
SPREAD 12in (30cm)	
SITE Full sun	
SOIL Rich in organic matter, sandy, free-draining	
HARDINESS Z9–10	
FLOWERING Summer	

Amaryllis belladonna

THE STRONG, UPRIGHT STEMS of *Amaryllis belladonna* have about six trumpet-shaped, scented pink flowers that are followed by glossy leaves. These leaves are strap-shaped and grow up to 16in (40cm) long. The tall, bare, thick flower stems can be partly hidden by other planting—for example, an adjacent salvia or short, hardy fuschia. Make sure the bulbs are planted in average, free-draining soil in a sunny, sheltered, frost-free place. Beware of slugs, and note that the hippeastrum/amaryllis houseplants commonly sold are completely different. Keep *A. belladonna* away from orange-colored backgrounds so that the pink flowers really stand out.

OTHER VARIETY *A. belladonna* 'Johannesburg' (pale pink flowers).

PLANT PROFILE	
HEIGHT	24in (60cm)
SPREAD	4in (10cm)
SITE	Full sun
SOIL	Average, free-draining
HARDINESS	Z7–11 H12–7
FLOWERING	Autumn

A

Anemone blanda 'White Splendour' Greek windflower

AN INVALUABLE SPRING PLANT (in mild weather it may even flower at the end of winter), *Anemone blanda* 'White Splendour' makes a brilliant show of star-shaped, white flowers above cut-leaved foliage. It quickly forms small clumps and spreads, creating lovely drifts. The large flowers mix particularly well with blue scillas in grass under magnolias, such as *M. stellata*. Although it might seem like a good idea to plant 'White Splendour' next to a contrastingly colored form such as the magenta 'Radar', it is better to keep different groups apart or seedlings will cross-breed and emerge in less striking, in-between colors. Grow in free-draining, rich soil.

OTHER VARIETY *A. blanda* 'Charmer' (deep pink flowers).

PLANT PROFILE
HEIGHT 6in (15cm)
SPREAD 6in (15cm)
SITE Sun or partial shade
SOIL Rich in organic matter, free-draining, light, sandy
HARDINESS Z4–8 H8–1
FLOWERING Spring

Anemone coronaria De Caen Group 'Mister Fokker' Windflower

TO CREATE SUCCESFUL CLUMPS of *Anemone coronaria* De Caen Group 'Mister Fokker', give the bulbs a sheltered position where they can bake in the summer sun—the wild form comes from the Mediterranean. The ground needs to have excellent drainage, which rules out heavy, sticky clay. It also helps if you provide a thick winter mulch to keep out the cold. Aside from this violet-blue-flowered variety of *A. coronaria*, there are many other forms in other colors, also with finely divided, carrot- or parsleylike leaves. They can be kept separate or mixed for a colorful tapestry effect.

OTHER VARIETY *A. coronaria* De Caen Group 'Lord Lieutenant' (deep blue flowers).

PLANT PROFILE	
HEIGHT 12–18in (30–45cm)	
SPREAD 6in (15cm)	
SITE Full sun	
SOIL Light, sandy	
HARDINESS Z8–11 H12–8	
FLOWERING Spring	

Anemone x *fulgens* Scarlet windflower

THE SCARLET FLOWERS of *Anemone* x *fulgens* are as brilliant as those
of the brightest, reddest poppy, and open in early spring. They
mix well with the 4in- (10cm-) high, semiprostrate, green-yellow–
flowering *Euphorbia myrsinites*, which also flowers in spring. In the
wild, this windflower grows in Greece and Turkey, in hot, sunny,
free-draining sites, and that is exactly what it likes in the garden,
along with a chance to bake over summer. Pile a thick mulch of
compost on top of the soil over winter to help insulate the plant
against the cold.

OTHER VARIETY *A.* x *fulgens* 'Annulata Grandiflora' (red flowers with
yellow centers).

PLANT PROFILE
HEIGHT 12in (30cm)
SPREAD 6in (15cm)
SITE Full sun
SOIL Light, sandy, free-draining
HARDINESS Z8–11 H12–8
FLOWERING Spring or early summer

Anemone pavonina Windflower

A

THE LARGE FLOWERS of *Anemone pavonina* are usually bright red
and have a white or yellow eye, but to get the best out of them you
will definitely need a hot, sunny site. In the wild it grows in stony
ground in the Mediterranean. In the garden it therefore needs free-
draining, sandy soil, and a chance to bake over summer. It mixes
well with thymes. The St. Bavo Group has large flowers in shades
of purple, pink, and salmon-pink.

OTHER VARIETY *A. pavonina* var. *ocellata* (scarlet with white centers).

PLANT PROFILE
HEIGHT 10in (25cm)
SPREAD 6in (15cm)
SITE Full sun
SOIL Light, sandy, free-draining
HARDINESS Z8–10 H10–8
FLOWERING Early spring

A | *Anomatheca laxa* False freesia

ORIGINALLY FROM SOUTH AFRICA, *Anomatheca laxa* produces swordlike leaves, up to 14in (35cm) long, and stems, usually of equal height, with small, trumpet-shaped red flowers. It needs a sunny, sheltered, frost-free position in free-draining, sandy soil. The name *anomatheca* means "irregular capsule" because that is how the cover of the brown autumn seed capsule was regarded; the seeds are bright red. It will occasionally withstand winter temperatures diving down as low as 23°F (−5°C).

OTHER VARIETY *A. laxa* var. *alba* (pure white flowers).

PLANT PROFILE	
HEIGHT 6–12in (15–30cm)	
SPREAD 2in (5cm)	
SITE Full sun	
SOIL Average, free-draining, sandy	
HARDINESS Z8–10	
FLOWERING Early summer	

Babiana stricta Baboon flower

B

THERE ARE OVER 20 DIFFERENT wild forms of the South African babiana, including the pretty *Babiana rubrocyanea* (*see inset*), and while not widely available, they can be found through specialists. So far, the best one is *B. stricta*. Its long flowering period produces blooms with a dark red center. A deep autumn planting, 8in (20cm) underground, and thick winter mulch will act as a blanket. Soil must be light, rich, and free-draining. In gardens where temperatures rarely hit 23°F (−5°C), it might thrive outside; otherwise, it should be grown inside in pots.

OTHER VARIETY *B. nana* (blue, lilac, or pink flowers with white and mauve or yellow).

PLANT PROFILE	
HEIGHT 4–12in (10–30cm)	
SPREAD 2in (5cm)	
SITE Full sun	
SOIL Fertile, light, free-draining	
HARDINESS Z13–15 H12–10	
FLOWERING Spring	

B

Begonia 'Anniversary'

PLANT THE TUBERS of *Begonia* 'Anniversary' hollow side up in pots in a greenhouse in spring, keeping them at a temperature of 60–64°F (16–18°C), and they should be at their peak in five months. Don't plant them outside until late spring, after the last frost, in fertile, neutral to acidic, free-draining soil; water them well in summer. Either discard the bulbs in the autumn or dig them up before the first frosts. Then cut back the stems, leaving 6in (15cm), and place on trays in a cool, dry shed. When dry, remove the soil and roots, and store in wooden boxes at just under 45°F (7°C). Alternatively, buy a ready-grown plant or treat it as an annual. Best planted toward the front of a border where there is partial shade.

OTHER VARIETY *B.* 'Jean Blair' (yellow flowers with a red edge).

PLANT PROFILE

HEIGHT 24in (60cm)

SPREAD 18in (45cm)

SITE Partial shade

SOIL Fertile, free-draining, neutral to slightly acidic

HARDINESS Min 50°F (10°C)

FLOWERING Summer

Begonia 'Apricot Delight'

B

SOME BEGONIAS ARE SPECIALLY BRED to be bright and breezy, with upbeat, in-your-face colors. 'Apricot Delight', however, is a quiet and pale apricot orange. The good-sized flowers are 7in (17cm) wide, with overlapping petals. See 'Anniversary' (*opposite*) for full growing tips, but if all that sounds too intimidating, simply grow 'Apricot Delight' as an annual, buying ready-grown plants from garden centers in the spring. Acclimatize them by standing them outside on warm, sunny days, always bringing them in at night until there are no more freezing temperatures.

OTHER VARIETY *B.* 'Allan Langdon' (deep, rich red flowers).

PLANT PROFILE
HEIGHT 24in (60cm)
SPREAD 18in (45cm)
SITE Partial shade
SOIL Fertile, free-draining, neutral to slightly acidic
HARDINESS Min 50°F (10°C)
FLOWERING Early summer to midautumn

B | *Begonia* 'Billie Langdon'

A HIGHLY EFFECTIVE, free-flowering begonia, 'Billie Langdon' has large white flowers, 7in (18cm) wide, and overlapping, oval petals up to 8in (20cm) long. Like many begonias, it needs to be planted in decent groups for maximum impact; either keep all the whites together or mix them up with other colors to give a jamboree effect. 'Billie Langdon' can be grown toward the front of a border, or used as edging around an island bed with contrasting, richer colors behind it. See 'Anniversary' (*page 36*) for full growing tips.

OTHER VARIETY B. 'Thurstonii' (pink flowers).

PLANT PROFILE
HEIGHT 24in (60cm)
SPREAD 18in (45cm)
SITE Partial shade
SOIL Fertile, free-draining, neutral to slightly acidic
HARDINESS Z13–15 H12–1
FLOWERING Summer

B

Begonia 'Can-can'

AN EXQUISITE, YELLOW-FLOWERING BEGONIA, 'Can-can' has a thin red band running all around the tips of the petals, giving an added attraction. The flowers are 7in (18cm) wide, and the leaves are 8in (20cm) long. It is definitely on the showy side, and can either be grown to flesh out a wide range of border schemes or to highlight and embellish a prominent feature, such as a statue or plinth. 'Can-can' also makes a highly effective, beautiful plant for edging the length of a path. For full growing tips, see 'Anniversary' (*page 36*).

OTHER VARIETY *B.* 'Fairylight' (white flowers with a red edge).

PLANT PROFILE
HEIGHT 3ft (1m)
SPREAD 18in (45cm)
SITE Partial shade
SOIL Fertile, free-draining, neutral to slightly acidic
HARDINESS Z13–15 H12–1
FLOWERING Summer

B

Begonia 'Flamboyant'

ONE OF THE BEST of the dark red begonias, 'Flamboyant' certainly
lives up to its name. It is highly rated because it keeps flowering
over summer without any pampering. Because it is significantly
shorter than many begonias and has attractive, heart-shaped leaves,
it's an excellent choice for the front of a border. 'Flamboyant' can
also be grown in large containers or pots, with taller bright yellows
and blues behind. Grow as for 'Anniversary' (*see page 36*).

PLANT PROFILE

HEIGHT 7in (17cm)

SPREAD 6in (15cm)

SITE Partial shade

SOIL Fertile, free-draining,
neutral to slightly acidic

HARDINESS Z13–15
H12–1

FLOWERING Summer

Begonia grandis subsp. *evansiana* var. *alba* Hardy begonia

B

A GOOD CHOICE if you want a smaller-flowering, more natural-looking begonia than those with highly bred, massive, brightly colored blooms. The scented pink or white flowers blend nicely with the olive green leaves (sometimes red beneath), and provide a good scattering of color over the summer months in cottage gardens. It can also be grown in relatively informal oriental designs because its parent comes from the Far East. 'Claret Jug' has pink flowers and leaves with a red tinge underneath. See 'Anniversary' (*page 36*) for full growing tips.

OTHER VARIETY B. *dregei* (white flowers).

PLANT PROFILE

HEIGHT 20in (50cm)

SPREAD 12in (30cm)

SITE Partial shade

SOIL Fertile, free-draining, neutral to slightly acidic

HARDINESS Z6–9

FLOWERING Summer

B | *Begonia* 'Illumination Orange'

THIS ATTRACTIVE SERIES INCLUDES flowers in apricot, pink, salmon, and white, and the orange of *Begonia* 'Illumination Orange' is brilliantly bright and vivid. Its showy blooms are 3in (8cm) wide, and are produced in arching cascades that make it a particularly good choice for pots or hanging baskets. It can also be grown at the front of a bed, which is fine if the flowers fall onto a paved path, but if they spill onto the lawn it will be tricky to mow the grass without decapitating the stems. See 'Anniversary' (*page 36*) for full growing tips.

OTHER VARIETY *B.* 'Illumination White' (pure white flowers).

PLANT PROFILE
HEIGHT 24in (60cm)
SPREAD 12in (30cm)
SITE Partial shade
SOIL Fertile, free-draining, neutral to slightly acidic
HARDINESS H12–1
FLOWERING Summer

Begonia Non Stop Series

RELATIVELY NEAT AND COMPACT, begonias in the Non Stop Series have attractive, heart-shaped leaves that are 4–6in (10–15cm) long, as well as 3in- (8cm-) wide, camellia-like flowers. The series name accurately suggests that the plants are a good buy, and you certainly get a regular supply of blooms all through the summer. Plants flower in various colors, including red, yellow, apricot, orange, pink, and white, and are often used to edge beds and borders in formal and informal gardens. For more information see 'Anniversary' (*page 36*).

OTHER VARIETY *B.* 'Festiva' (yellow flowers).

PLANT PROFILE
HEIGHT 12in (30cm)
SPREAD 12in (30cm)
SITE Partial shade
SOIL Fertile, free-draining, neutral to slightly acidic
HARDINESS Z13–15 H12–1
FLOWERING Summer

B | *Begonia* 'Orange Cascade'

THE CASCADE SERIES is an excellent choice for pots or hanging baskets because its branching stems arch over the sides, giving nicely rounded growth. *Begonia* 'Orange Cascade' gives a profuse show of bright, boisterous, orange flowers all summer, and makes a particularly effective filler if any gaps suddenly appear near the front of a border. Place with care, keeping it well away from soft, pastel-colored flowers because they will be visually overpowered. See 'Anniversary' (*page 36*) for full growing tips.

OTHER VARIETY *B.* 'Crimson Cascade' (bright red flowers).

PLANT PROFILE
HEIGHT 24in (60cm)
SPREAD 24in (60cm)
SITE Partial shade
SOIL Fertile, free-draining, neutral to slightly acidic
HARDINESS Z13–15 H12–1
FLOWERING Summer

Begonia 'Roy Hartley'

A THOROUGHLY RELIABLE VARIETY, *Begonia* 'Roy Hartley' has soft pink flowers. They are 4in (10cm) wide, nicely rounded, and give a long show all summer. Use it in pastel gardens, but note that in full sun the pink will tend to bleach out, while in sites with some shade during the day it will be slightly richer. 'Roy Hartley' goes well with pale blues and peachy colors, and looks good next to dark green leaves. For full growing tips, see 'Anniversary' (*page 36*).

OTHER VARIETY *B*. 'Primrose' (pale yellow flowers).

PLANT PROFILE	
HEIGHT 24in (60cm)	
SPREAD 18in (45cm)	
SITE Partial shade	
SOIL Fertile, free-draining, neutral to slightly acidic	
HARDINESS Z13–15 H12–1	
FLOWERING Summer	

B | *Bellevalia paradoxa* Sicilian bulb

SOMETIMES SOLD AS *Bellevalia pycnantha*, *B. paradoxa* is a superb and highly unusual little plant with dark, navy blue flowers and a yellow-white rim. The buds are initially tightly packed together on top of the flower spike, making a conical shape, and slowly start opening from the bottom up. Make sure it is planted in groups near the front of a border where it can be seen clearly. Plant the bulbs 4in (10cm) deep in the autumn in free-draining soil; they like to be on the dry side over summer. Beware of slugs attacking the leaves.

OTHER VARIETY *B. romana* (white flowers).

PLANT PROFILE	
HEIGHT 12in (30cm)	
SPREAD 2in (5cm)	
SITE Full sun	
SOIL Free-draining	
HARDINESS Z7–9 H9–7	
FLOWERING Spring	

Bletilla striata Chinese ground orchid

B

ONE OF THE FEW ORCHIDS that can be grown outdoors in winter in mild areas, *Bletilla striata* is not hardy and needs plenty of pampering. In return, it produces an extremely attractive five-petaled, magenta flower with a protruding lip. Fertile, moist but free-draining soil is essential, as is a sheltered position. It can be left outside all year in mild gardens if the crown is given a thick, protective covering of mulch. If in any doubt, carefully dig it up in autumn, pot it, and keep it under glass over winter, planting out again when temperatures pick up in early summer. *B. striata* can also be grown in a large pot and moved outside in the summer.

OTHER VARIETY *B. striata alba* (white flowers).

PLANT PROFILE

HEIGHT 12–24in (30–60cm)

SITE Partial shade

SOIL Fertile, moist but free-draining

HARDINESS Z5–8 H8–5

FLOWERING Spring to early summer

B | *Brimeura amethystina* Spanish hyacinth

A SMALL, DELICATE ALTERNATIVE to bluebells, the rarely grown *Brimeura amethystina* has pale to dark blue flowers. It is worth growing for its tubular, bell-shaped blooms, which appear on top of short spikes set among narrow, bright green leaves. The bulbs are a good choice for cool, lightly shaded parts of the garden, planted, for example, with small-leaved hostas that flower several weeks before the brimeura. Plant the bulbs 2in (5cm) deep in the autumn. In the wild, it is found in the Pyrenees, so it's a good choice for rock gardens and raised beds with excellent drainage.

OTHER VARIETY *B. amethystina* 'Alba' (white flowers).

PLANT PROFILE

HEIGHT 4–8in (10–20cm)

SPREAD 2in (5cm)

SITE Partial shade

SOIL Rich in organic matter, free-draining

HARDINESS Z5–9 H9–5

FLOWERING Spring

Brodiaea californica

A DELIGHTFUL CALIFORNIA PLANT, *Brodiaea californica* gives clusters of small, violet, lilac, or pink flowers on thin wiry stems. It blooms at the end of spring and into early summer. The display is quietly attractive, and adds an extra layer of interest after the main spring display and before the main summer borders start revving up. *B. californica* can also be grown in rock gardens. Plant corms in groups in the autumn, 3in (8cm) deep, in light, sandy soil. Water well in growth, and let the plants bake while dormant in summer. In frost-prone areas, protect the ground with a thick winter mulch.

OTHER VARIETY *B. elegans* (funnel-shaped, deep purple flowers).

PLANT PROFILE

HEIGHT 20in (50cm)

SPREAD 3in (8cm)

SITE Full sun or partial shade

SOIL Fertile, free-draining, light, sandy loam

HARDINESS Z8–10

FLOWERING Early summer

B | *Bulbocodium vernum* Spring meadow saffron

JUST LIKE A LARGE CROCUS or colchicum, the pink–purple flowers of *Bulbocodium vernum* look as if they have burst straight out of the soil—they sit with their base on the ground, their petals pointing upward and outward. They add a quiet, attractive note and are about 1⅓in (4cm) wide, and usually followed by three leaves, which reach their maximum length of 6in (15cm) soon after. The best site is in a rock garden where the flowers can be clearly seen and there is excellent drainage, or in a patch of not-too-vigorous grass. In the autumn, plant the corms 3in (8cm) deep in rich soil.

PLANT PROFILE

HEIGHT 1½–3in (4–8cm)

SPREAD 2in (5cm)

SITE Full sun

SOIL Rich in organic matter, free-draining

HARDINESS Z7–9 H9–7

FLOWERING Spring

Calochortus venustus Fairy lantern

C

THIS CALOCHORTUS has bowl-shaped flowers, often in quite striking colors. The most eye-catching kinds of *C. venustus* are dark red, but all have a yellow-ringed, dark red mark inside as well. They provide a lively link between the spring flowers and the early summer show. Provide extremely free-draining soil, with plenty of added horticultural sand if necessary. Do not water after flowering because the dormant bulbs prefer to be kept dry—to be on the safe side, dig them up and keep them dry in a cool, airy place for planting out again in the autumn.

OTHER VARIETY *C. superbus* (cup-shaped, white, cream, lavender-blue or yellow flowers).

PLANT PROFILE	
HEIGHT 8–24in (20–60cm)	
SPREAD 3in (8cm)	
SITE Full sun	
SOIL Free-draining, sandy, loam	
HARDINESS Z6–10 H10–6	
FLOWERING Late spring to summer	

C | *Camassia cusickii* Quamash

THE SMALL, STEEL BLUE BLOOMS of *Camassia cusickii* (which make good cut flowers) appear on the top half of vertical stems. They give a light, airy effect, but need to be grown in clumps and set against a darkish background to be clearly seen. *C. cusickii* can also be grown in a wild garden. The fresh green leaves are long, thin, and straplike, and tend to bend down to the ground. It does not need pampering, and grows in average garden soil as long as it is neither too free-draining nor heavy and waterlogged. In areas with cold winters, provide some insulation with a thick winter mulch of compost.

OTHER VARIETY *C. cusickii* 'Zwanenburg' (deep blue flowers).

PLANT PROFILE

HEIGHT 24–32in (60–80cm)

SPREAD 4in (10cm)

SITE Sun or partial shade

SOIL Fertile, rich in organic matter, moist but free-draining

HARDINESS Z3–11 H12–1

FLOWERING Late spring

Camassia leichtlinii Quamash

C

ALSO AVAILABLE IN STRIKING VARIATIONS of blue and brilliant purple, the star-shaped flowers of *Camassia leichtlinii* appear on the top half of upright stems and are usually creamy white, as are those of *C. leichtlinii* subsp. *leichtlinii*, and it can be difficult to distinguish between the two. Best grown in clumps to create a strong effect, it is excellent in both borders and wild gardens. Avoid parts of the garden that tend to be very dry or very wet. Because this group of camassias flowers in late spring and dies down at the start of summer, it is a good idea to grow a summer-flowering plant nearby.

OTHER VARIETY *C. leichtlinii* subsp. *suksdorfii* (blue to violet flowers).

PLANT PROFILE

HEIGHT 3ft (1m)

SPREAD 4in (10cm)

SITE Sun or partial shade

SOIL Fertile, rich in organic matter, moist but free-draining

HARDINESS Z4–10 H10–1

FLOWERING Late spring

C *Canna* 'Endeavour' Indian shot plant

A TALL AND FLAMBOYANT PLANT, *Canna* 'Endeavour' reaches well over head height and is ideal for the back of borders or the center of island beds where the bright, soft red flowers can perch above long, lush, paddlelike leaves. Fertile soil and regular watering in dry summer spells are vital. Dig it up after the first autumn frost, cut off the blackened top growth, place the thick, fleshy, bulblike structure in a wooden box filled with bark, and keep it in a frost-free place over winter. Give it an occasional drink to prevent the roots from shriveling and dying.

OTHER VARIETY *C.* 'Wyoming' (brown–purple leaves, orange flowers).

PLANT PROFILE
HEIGHT 5–7ft (1.5–2.2m)
SPREAD 20in (50cm)
SITE Full sun
SOIL Fertile
HARDINESS Z8–11
FLOWERING Midsummer to early autumn

Canna 'Striata' Indian shot plant

CANNAS ADD A STRIKING TOUCH to any garden, and *C.* 'Striata' is one of the experts' favorites because of its bright variegated leaves and contrasting, small, gladiolus-like orange flowers perched on top of the flower spike. The giant, paddlelike leaves have highly distinctive yellow veins. For the best effect, place 'Striata' where the sun will shine though the leaves. Fertile soil and regular watering in dry spells are vital. Dig up after the first light frost, cut off the top growth, and keep dry over winter. In late autumn, place the rhizome in a wooden box filled with barely moist bark, and store in a frost free place. Pot next spring for planting out in early summer.

OTHER VARIETY *C.* 'Black Knight' (very dark red flowers).

PLANT PROFILE
HEIGHT 5ft (1.5m)
SPREAD 20in (50cm)
SITE Full sun
SOIL Fertile
HARDINESS Z8–11 H12–1
FLOWERING Midsummer to early autumn

C | *Cardiocrinum giganteum* Giant lily

PLANT PROFILE

ONE OF THE MOST DRAMATIC PLANTS in the garden, *Cardiocrinum giganteum* sends up a fantastically vigorous flower stem that really can hit 12ft (4m) high. Up to 20 large, white, richly scented flowers appear at the top of this stem above the glossy, dark green leaves. Plant bulbs just under the soil surface in the autumn, in cool, light shade. The soil should be moist (even in summer), fertile, and free-draining. In summer, water whenever the soil threatens to turn dry, and apply liquid fertilizer two or three times to encourage the growth of replacement bulbs (the parent dies after flowering). The young bulbs will take a few years to flower.

OTHER VARIETY *C. giganteum* var. *yunnanense* (green-tinted flowers).

HEIGHT	5–12ft (1.5–4m)
SPREAD	18in (45cm)
SITE	Partial shade
SOIL	Fertile, rich in organic matter, moist but free-draining
HARDINESS	Z7–9 H9–7
FLOWERING	Summer

Chionodoxa luciliae Glory of the snow

THIS GLORY OF THE SNOW adds an extremely useful spread of star-shaped, soft blue flowers with white centers in early spring, and is a good choice for parts of the garden with dappled summer shade. Plant the bulbs in rock gardens or under deciduous trees and shrubs (roses, for example) to flower before the leaves start screening out the bright sun. Each flower spreads seed, creating extra plants. Plant the bulbs close together in the autumn in a sunny position, but don't let them become excessively dry over the summer.

OTHER VARIETY *C. forbesii* (star-shaped blue flowers).

PLANT PROFILE
HEIGHT 6in (15cm)
SPREAD 1¼in (3cm)
SITE Full sun or dappled shade
SOIL Free-draining
HARDINESS Z3–9 H9–1
FLOWERING Early spring

C | *Chionodoxa* 'Pink Giant' Glory of the snow

THE WHITE-CENTERED FLOWERS of *Chionodoxa* 'Pink Giant', sometimes sold as *C. forbesii* 'Pink Giant', look like little stars and make a small, gentle show in early spring—they are ½in (1.5cm) wide, with up to 12 flowers per stem. It is best planted around deciduous shrubs where it will get plenty of sun in spring and shade in summer, when it must not be allowed to bake dry. After a few years, more plants will sprout up from the scattered seed. A good alternative is *C. luciliae*, which has just one to three, slightly larger blue flowers that also appear in early spring. Plant the bulbs in autumn in light shade, and water the soil in summer when hot and dry.

OTHER VARIETY *C. forbesii* 'Blue Giant' (large blue flowers).

PLANT PROFILE	
HEIGHT 4–8in (10–20cm)	
SPREAD 1¼in (3cm)	
SITE Full sun	
SOIL Free-draining	
HARDINESS Z3–9 H9–1	
FLOWERING Early spring	

Chionodoxa sardensis Glory of the snow

WITH THE STRONGEST BLUE of any of the chionodoxas, albeit slightly smaller than *Chionodoxa forbesii* and *C. luciliae*, this native of mountainous western Turkey puts on a fine show. It freely sets seed and spreads, making attractive clumps. Use the bulbs in rock gardens or under deciduous trees and shrubs to flower before the leaves start screening out the bright sun. Plant the bulbs close together in autumn in a sunny position, but don't let them become excessively dry over the summer. Water the soil if it becomes too parched.

OTHER VARIETY *C. forbesii* 'Alba' (bright white flowers).

PLANT PROFILE	
HEIGHT	4–8in (10–20cm)
SPREAD	1¼in (3cm)
SITE	Full sun
SOIL	Free-draining
HARDINESS	Z3–9 H9–1
FLOWERING	Early spring

C | *Chlidanthus fragrans*

UNLESS YOU HAVE A REMARKABLY warm and sheltered garden, this South American bulb (from the Peruvian Andes) can be grown in a conservatory, though the pots can be inserted into a flower bed over summer. That is when they produce clusters of three to five, strongly scented, trumpet-shaped, golden yellow flowers, each being 2in (5cm) wide. The gray-green leaves can reach 16in (40cm) long. Plant the bulbs in spring with the nose just above the soil surface, using a loam-based potting mix. Water freely in growth, reducing the quantities as the leaves start to wither. Keep cool and dry, under cover, over winter.

PLANT PROFILE

HEIGHT 12in (30cm)

SPREAD 3in (8cm)

SITE Sheltered

SOIL Loam-based potting mix

HARDINESS Z12–15 H12–7

FLOWERING Summer

Colchicum agrippinum Autumn crocus

C

IN THE EARLY AUTUMN, *Colchicum agrippinum* produces large, crocuslike flowers at soil level (although the crocus comparison tends to infuriate experts, because botanically crocuses are very different). The flowers' attraction lies in the checkered patterning on their purple-pink petals. The foliage appears in early spring and dies at the start of summer. In full sun and good soil, which must not be too dry, the bulbs multiply, giving a spreading show of color, and for this reason they are popularly grown in grass. All parts of the plant are highly toxic, and skin contact can lead to irritation.

OTHER VARIETY *C. autumnale* (lavender-pink flowers).

PLANT PROFILE

HEIGHT 3–4in (8–10cm)

SPREAD 3in (8cm)

SITE Full sun

SOIL Fertile, moist but free-draining

HARDINESS Z4–9 H9–1

FLOWERING Early autumn

C | *Colchicum speciosum* 'Album' Autumn crocus

IF YOU ONLY BUY ONE KIND of colchicum, make it *C. speciosum* 'Album' because the white flowers are large, goblet-shaped, and robust, and they won't be beaten down and ruined by rain. 'Album' can be grown in rich, free-draining soil that never gets too dry, or planted in grass, though the results might be disappointing because it might not spread very well. The purple-pink *C. speciosum* goes well with the striking red, poisonous autumn berries of the 10in- (25cm-) high *Arum italicum* 'Marmoratum' and the 18in (45cm) *Iris foetidissima*.

OTHER VARIETY *C. cilicicum* (funnel-shaped, purple-pink flowers).

PLANT PROFILE

HEIGHT 7in (18cm)

SPREAD 4in (10cm)

SITE Full sun

SOIL Fertile, moist but free-draining

HARDINESS Z4–9 H9–1

FLOWERING Autumn

Colchicum 'Waterlily' Autumn crocus

C

THE DOUBLE, PINK-LILAC *Colchicum* 'Waterlily' is one of the showiest of the autumn crocuses and is an extremely useful, if small, addition to the great explosion of autumn colors. Its only drawback is that the short stems are not quite strong enough to keep the flowers upright, but you can easily overcome this by making sure that neighboring plants provide some support. Lilac-pink 'Lilac Wonder' is slightly more robust and much less likely to keel over, especially after heavy rain. Grow 'Waterlily' in good soil that never gets too dry.

OTHER VARIETY *C.* 'Rosy Dawn' (fragrant, pink-violet flowers).

PLANT PROFILE
HEIGHT 5in (12cm)
SPREAD 4in (10cm)
SITE Full sun
SOIL Fertile, moist but free-draining
HARDINESS Z4–9 H9–1
FLOWERING Autumn

C

Crinum x *powellii* 'Album' Swamp lily

A DUAL-PURPOSE BULB, *Crinum* x *powellii* 'Album' can be grown in borders or in the shallows of a pond. There are clusters of up to ten scented, widely flared flowers, while the leaves grow up to 5ft (1.5m) long. Many rate 'Album' much more highly than its pale pink parent *C.* x *powellii* (*see inset*) because the pure white flowers have much more impact. Plant the bulbs with the nose just above soil level. The ground should be fertile, and moist but free-draining. Water well in full growth. Beware of contact with the skin because it can cause irritation.

OTHER VARIETY *C. moorei* (flowers are white or shades of pink).

PLANT PROFILE

HEIGHT 5ft (1.5m)

SPREAD 12in (30cm)

SITE Full sun

SOIL Fertile, rich in organic matter, moist but free-draining

HARDINESS Z7–11 H12–8

FLOWERING Late summer to autumn

Crocus ancyrensis

C

ONE OF THE EARLIEST CROCUSES to flower in the New Year, *C. ancyrensis* has five or more bright yellow or orange flowers. Crocuses generally need a bright sunny position and good drainage. Plant spring-flowerers like this one in autumn, and the autumn-flowering kind in late summer, 3in (8cm) deep, at the front of borders or in rock gardens. When planting in drifts in grass, cut out three sides of a square on the ground, going through the sod. Peel it back, lightly prong the soil if compacted, scatter the corms about 3in (8cm) apart, adding a bit of bone meal, and firm down the turf. Do not mow the area until the leaves have died back because they help build up crucial energy supplies for next year's display.

OTHER VARIETY *C. dalmaticus* (pale lilac flowers).

PLANT PROFILE

HEIGHT 2in (5cm)

SPREAD 2in (5cm)

SITE Full sun

SOIL Sandy, poor to average, free-draining

HARDINESS Z3–8 H8–1

FLOWERING Late winter and early spring

C | *Crocus angustifolius* Cloth-of-gold crocus

BRIGHT AND SHOWY, the cloth-of-gold crocus looks best when it has multiplied to create a large spread of bulbs flaring their orange-yellow flowers. On closer inspection, you'll see that the outsides of the petals are marked, and often striped, with an attractive bronze color. *Crocus angustifolius* can also be used to great effect in quite small gardens, and when planted in clusters it will lead the eye around the design, giving the illusion of greater space. For full growing tips see *C. ancyrensis (page 65)*.

OTHER VARIETY *C. biflorus* (yellow-throated flowers in shades of lilac-blue or white, sometimes striped purple or brown-purple).

PLANT PROFILE		
HEIGHT 2in (5cm)		
SPREAD 2in (5cm)		
SITE Full sun		
SOIL Sandy, poor to average, free-draining		
HARDINESS Z3–8 H8–1		
FLOWERING Spring		

Crocus banaticus

C

FLOWERING IN EARLY TO MIDAUTUMN, *Crocus banaticus* can be grown in light shade and is very highly rated because its flowers look a bit like miniature irises. There are three large outer petals measuring about 2in (5cm) long, and three inner ones pointing upright. This crocus is excellent for growing in drifts at the front of a border, but you must not let it get swamped by larger plants. Moist but free-draining ground in a cool, lightly shaded position is ideal. See *C. ancyrensis* (*page 65*) for more information.

OTHER VARIETY *C. hadriaticus* (white flowers).

PLANT PROFILE

HEIGHT 4in (10cm)

SPREAD 2in (5cm)

SITE Sun or partial shade

SOIL Average, rich in organic matter, moist but free-draining

HARDINESS Z3–8 H8–1

FLOWERING Early autumn

C | *Crocus chrysanthus* 'Gipsy Girl'

LARGE, VIGOROUS, AND ATTRACTIVE, *Crocus chrysanthus* 'Gipsy Girl' has purple stripes and markings on the outside of the petals, and spreads to make a colorful clump in grass. It can be grown alone or mixed with similar chrysanthus hybrids to make a patchwork quilt effect on the lawn. They will interbreed to create some winners and some losers. Grow in poor to average, free-draining soil. For more information about growing, see *C. ancyrensis* (*page 65*).

OTHER VARIETY *C. chrysanthus* 'Blue Pearl' (yellow-throated white flowers, with soft lilac-blue).

PLANT PROFILE

HEIGHT 3in (7cm)

SPREAD 2in (5cm)

SITE Full sun

SOIL Poor to average, sandy, free-draining

HARDINESS Z3–8 H8–1

FLOWERING Spring

Crocus chrysanthus 'Ladykiller'

C

THE FLOWERS OF THIS PLANT are white inside, with deep purple markings on the outside, making an eye-catching contrast. *Crocus chrysanthus* 'Ladykiller' can be grown alone or mixed with other chrysanthus hybrids, such as *C. chrysanthus* 'Snow Bunting' and the yellow *C. chrysanthus* 'Gipsy Girl', to great effect. They will interbreed with varying degrees of success. See *C. ancyrensis* (*page 65*) for full growing tips.

OTHER VARIETY *C. chrysanthus* 'Cream Beauty' (rich cream flowers with pale green-brown bases and deep golden yellow throats).

PLANT PROFILE
HEIGHT 3in (7cm)
SPREAD 2in (5cm)
SITE Full sun
SOIL Poor to average, sandy, free-draining
HARDINESS Z3–8 H8–1
FLOWERING Spring

C | *Crocus chrysanthus* 'Snow Bunting'

AS WHITE AS ITS NAME SUGGESTS, *Crocus chrysanthus* 'Snow Bunting' has a sweet scent and spreads to make decent clumps. It can be grown alone or mixed in grass with other chrysanthus hybrids, such as the pale blue 'Blue Bird' and the yellow 'Gipsy Girl' (*page 68*). If mixed, the different cultivars will interbreed to create some winners and some losers. For full growing tips, see *C. ancyrensis* (*page 65*).

OTHER VARIETY *C. chrysanthus* 'E.A. Bowles' (rich lemon yellow flowers with bronze-green bases and purple feathering).

PLANT PROFILE
HEIGHT 3in (7cm)
SPREAD 2in (5cm)
SITE Full sun
SOIL Poor to average, sandy, free-draining
HARDINESS Z3–8 H8–1
FLOWERING Spring

Crocus goulimyi

A GORGEOUS SIGHT IN SOUTHERN GREECE, where it turns the ground under olive trees lilac-blue, the scented flowers of *Crocus goulimyi* are shaped like goblets. They need full sun to thrive, and a sheltered part of the garden is best. In cool regions, *C. goulimyi* is often grown in sunny gravel or rock gardens where there is excellent drainage, or in Mediterranean-style courtyards where the walls create a sun-trap. If you cannot provide these conditions, grow a few bulbs in a trough or container that you can move into a greenhouse for the winter months. See *C. ancyrensis* (*page 65*) for more information.

OTHER VARIETY *C. kotschyanus* (pale lilac flowers).

PLANT PROFILE	
HEIGHT 4in (10cm)	
SPREAD 2in (5cm)	
SITE Full sun	
SOIL Poor to average, sandy, free-draining	
HARDINESS Z3–8 H8–1	
FLOWERING Autumn	

C | *Crocus medius*

THE RICH LILAC-PURPLE FLOWERS (though they can sometimes be paler), with a dash of bright orange-red in the middle, make *Crocus medius* an excellent choice for the garden. Plant it next to yellow daffodils or on its own in front of a white wall for contrast. In large spaces, grow it in large swaths around trees with superb white trunks (such as *Betula utilis* var. *jacquemontii* or *B. utilis* var. *jacquemontii* 'Grayswood Ghost'). The flowers appear just before the leaves. Make sure the site is sunny and free-draining. For full growing tips, see *C. ancyrensis* (*page 65*).

OTHER VARIETY *C. nudiflorus* (rich purple flowers).

PLANT PROFILE

HEIGHT 3in (8cm)

SPREAD 1in (2.5cm)

SITE Full sun

SOIL Poor to average, sandy, free-draining

HARDINESS Z3–8 H8–1

FLOWERING Late autumn

Crocus minimus

C

YOU WILL HAVE TO DRIVE AROUND CORSICA and Sardinia to see *Crocus minimus* in the wild, where it makes a beautiful show with its rich lilac purple flowers, and outer petals with darker violet markings. In cooler climates it is often grown in sunny rock gardens because it needs excellent drainage, or at the foot of a warm wall where it can bake over summer. Gravel and Mediterranean-style gardens provide equally good sites. Wherever it is grown, try to provide a contrasting white background. See *C. ancyrensis (page 65)* for full growing tips.

PLANT PROFILE
HEIGHT 3in (8cm)
SPREAD 1in (2.5cm)
SITE Full sun
SOIL Poor to average, sandy, free-draining
HARDINESS Z3–8 H8–1
FLOWERING Late spring

C | *Crocus ochroleucus*

WITH ITS YELLOW-THROATED, creamy white flowers, *Crocus ochroleucus* gives a bright show in late autumn before its leaves appear. It is a rampant spreader in grass, and looks good against trees with rich brown bark, such as the shiny *Prunus serrula*, and shrubs with dark green leaves. With a green thumb and a little luck, gardeners in mild climates can have crocuses in flower in different parts of the garden from late summer or early autumn right through to the start of the following summer. For more information about growing, see *C. ancyrensis* (*page 65*).

OTHER VARIETY *C. cartwrightianus* (lilac or white flowers).

PLANT PROFILE
HEIGHT 2in (5cm)
SPREAD 1in (2.5cm)
SITE Full sun
SOIL Poor to average, sandy, free-draining
HARDINESS Z5–8 H8–4
FLOWERING Late autumn

Crocus pulchellus

C

AN EXCELLENT WAY of brightening up the autumn and early winter garden, *Crocus pulchellus* provides attractive, goblet-shaped, pale lilac-blue flowers with violet veins and deep yellow throats. Plant it in drifts across the lawn or, better still, intermingle the bulbs with the slightly larger, violet-blue, autumn-flowering *C. speciosus*, with which it interbreeds, and then let nature take its course. The flowers also look attractive close to drifts of the rich purple *C. medius*. See *C. ancyrensis (page 65)* for full growing tips.

OTHER VARIETY *C. laevigatus* (white to lilac flowers).

PLANT PROFILE
HEIGHT 4–5in (10–12cm)
SPREAD 1½in (4cm)
SITE Full sun
SOIL Poor to average, sandy, free-draining
HARDINESS Z3–8 H8–1
FLOWERING Autumn to early winter

C

Crocus sieberi 'Albus'

THERE ARE ABOUT SEVEN DIFFERENT KINDS of the vigorous *Crocus sieberi*, and *C. sieberi* 'Albus' (previously called 'Bowles' White') is the the creamy version. The parent and its cultivars are among the best and liveliest early spring crocuses, and put on a vigorous show. Other forms offer violet flowers (*C. sieberi* 'Firefly' and *C. sieberi* 'Violet Queen'), while *C. sieberi* subsp. *sublimis* 'Tricolor' has bands of color. For full growing tips, see *C. ancyrensis* (*page 65*).

OTHER VARIETY *C. sieberi* 'Hubert Edelsten' (pale lilac flowers).

PLANT PROFILE

HEIGHT 2–3in (5–8cm)

SPREAD 1in (2.5cm)

SITE Full sun

SOIL Poor to average, sandy, free-draining

HARDINESS Z3–8 H8–1

FLOWERING Late winter to early spring

Crocus sieberi subsp. *sublimis* 'Tricolor'

C

WITH THREE BANDS OF COLOR, it might sound a bit garish, but *Crocus sieberi* subsp. *sublimis* 'Tricolor' is just what you need in late winter and early spring when the garden needs perking up. Each flower has lilac across the tops of the petals, then white in the middle and yellow in the throat. Plant drifts or clumps wherever the garden looks a bit dull, and add some *C. sieberi* 'Albus' nearby for a lively contrast. They can all be followed by Dutch crocus (*C. vernus*), such as 'Jeanne d'Arc' (*page 81*), to keep the display going through spring. See *C. ancyrensis* (*page 65*) for full growing tips.

OTHER VARIETY *C. sieberi* 'Violet Queen' (deep violet flowers).

PLANT PROFILE

HEIGHT 1½in (4cm)

SPREAD 1in (2.5cm)

SITE Full sun

SOIL Poor to average, sandy, free-draining

HARDINESS Z3–8 H8–1

FLOWERING Late winter to early spring

C | *Crocus tommasinianus*

WITH AN EXTREMELY IMPRESSIVE runaway spread, unless it is
grown in vigorous grass, which keeps it in check (as do mice),
Crocus tommasinianus quickly multiplies and invades surrounding
space, creating sheets of silver-lilac to red-purple in late winter. For
that reason, it should always be kept out of borders, especially the
neat and organized kind, because it can become a nuisance. There
are many other attractive forms (*see opposite, and page 80*) that open
up their flowers when the wintry sun shines down. For fuller
information on growing, see *C. ancyrensis* (*page 65*).

OTHER VARIETY *C. tommasinianus* 'Barr's Purple' (purple flowers,
silvery outside).

PLANT PROFILE
HEIGHT 3–4in (8–10cm)
SPREAD 1in (2.5cm)
SITE Full sun
SOIL Poor to average, sandy, free-draining
HARDINESS Z3–8 H8–1
FLOWERING Late winter to spring

Crocus tommasinianus f. *albus*

C

A QUICK-SPREADING WHITE CROCUS, *C. tommasinianus* f. *albus* multiplies vigorously, making it a big bonus in large, open lawns and orchards and, conversely, a major nuisance in formal beds and borders, where it should never be grown. It is equally impressive whether planted as an all-white spread or when contrasted with the red-purple *C. tommasinianus* 'Whitewell Purple', which spreads just as vigorously. The two can be intermingled for a speckled effect or kept well apart in separate, contrasting clumps. See *C. ancyrensis* (*page 65*) for full growing tips.

OTHER VARIETY *C. tommasinianus* 'Lilac Beauty' (lilac flowers).

PLANT PROFILE	
HEIGHT 3–4in (8–10cm)	
SPREAD 1in (2.5cm)	
SITE Full sun	
SOIL Poor to average, sandy, free-draining	
HARDINESS Z3–8 H8–1	
FLOWERING Late winter to spring	

C *Crocus tommasinianus* 'Ruby Giant'

IF YOU WANT A REALLY STRONG-COLORED, fast-spreading crocus, go for *C. tommasinianus* 'Ruby Giant'. It produces rich red-purple flowers and looks good grown among trees with white trunks—for example, *Betula pendula* 'Laciniata'—and also makes a bright contrast with the white *C. tommasinianus* 'Eric Smith'. When grown around large ponds and white garden structures, including statues and greenhouses, it looks equally impressive. Given a mild spell in winter, the flowers quickly open. For full growing tips see *C. ancyrensis* (page 65).

OTHER VARIETY *C. tommasinianus* 'Whitewell Purple' (red-purple flowers, silver-mauve inside).

PLANT PROFILE	
HEIGHT	3–4in (8–10cm)
SPREAD	1in (2.5cm)
SITE	Full sun
SOIL	Poor to average, sandy, free-draining
HARDINESS	Z3–8 H8–1
FLOWERING	Late winter to spring

Crocus vernus subsp. *albiflorus* 'Jeanne d'Arc' Dutch crocus

C

DUTCH CROCUSES PROVIDE SPECTACULAR, dependable displays of color in the spring and are often seen in public gardens. The flowers are large and robust, and their colors usually range from lilac to shiny violet. They are ideal for planting in grass where they spread vigorously. *Crocus vernus* subsp. *albiflorus* 'Jeanne d'Arc' (sometimes sold as 'Joan of Arc') puts on a lovely show of white flowers with faint purple veining and deep purple at the base. Mixed with the pale blue 'Queen of the Blues', it creates a gentle, calming effect. See *C. ancyrensis* (*page 65*) for growing tips.

OTHER VARIETY *C. vernus* subsp. *albiflorus* 'Queen of the Blues' (lilac-blue flowers).

PLANT PROFILE
HEIGHT 4–5in (10–12cm)
SPREAD 2in (5cm)
SITE Full sun
SOIL Poor to average, sandy, free-draining
HARDINESS Z3–8 H8–1
FLOWERING Spring to early summer

C *Crocus vernus* subsp. *albiflorus* 'Pickwick' Dutch crocus

LIKE OTHER DUTCH CROCUSES, *C. vernus* subsp. *albiflorus* 'Pickwick' is a first-rate choice for planting in big, bold drifts in grass, where it quickly spreads. Its white flowers are heavily striped with pale and dark lilac, and have a dark purple base. Try growing 'Pickwick' with pastel-colored crocuses and others in richer colors to create a tapestry-like effect on a lawn, and to embellish stylish features such as fountains and statues, ornamental trees with brown or green trunks, and topiary hedges. For full growing tips, see *C. ancyrensis* (*page 65*).

OTHER VARIETY *C. vernus* subsp. *albiflorus* 'Remembrance' (shiny violet flowers).

PLANT PROFILE
HEIGHT 4–5in (10–12cm)
SPREAD 2in (5cm)
SITE Full sun
SOIL Poor to average, sandy, free-draining
HARDINESS Z3–8 H8–1
FLOWERING Spring to early summer

C

Cyclamen hederifolium Sowbread

IF YOU HAVE A PATCH of free-draining ground under a tree, bulk it up with leaf mold and grow *Cyclamen hederifolium*. Its tubers look like wizened, flattened, corky discs with all the zest of an old chunk of ginger. But its leaves, which come in a great variety of shapes, are gorgeous from autumn until spring, and are ivylike with patterned silvery markings against a green background. The markings on *C. hederifolium* var. *hederifolium* f. *albiflorum* Bowles' Apollo Group are just about the best. Although the pink-flowered *C. hederifolium* comes from the Mediterranean, it withstands much colder weather and is a vigorous self-seeder.

OTHER VARIETY *C. graecum* (pink to carmine red, not quite hardy).

PLANT PROFILE

HEIGHT 4–5in (10–13cm)

SPREAD 6in (15cm)

SITE Partial shade

SOIL Average, rich in organic matter, free-draining

HARDINESS Z5–7 H9–7

FLOWERING Mid- and late autumn

C | *Cyclamen repandum* subsp. *peloponnesiacum* Sowbread

AN EXCELLENT SPRING–FLOWERING CYCLAMEN for growing under deciduous trees in a semiwoodland site or in the sunny gaps between shrubs, *C. repandum* subsp. *peloponnesiacum* has three attractions. First, the quite large, almost triangular leaves are liberally covered with silver speckles; second, their edges are slightly wavy and scalloped; and, third, the pale pink flowers are nicely held up so that they can be seen clearly. It likes being kept on the dry side over summer, but it is not reliably hardy and needs a thick, protective covering of leaf mold in early winter.

OTHER VARIETY *C. repandum* (hardier, with gray-green speckled leaves and scented, deep, rich carmine red flowers).

PLANT PROFILE

HEIGHT 4–6in (10–15cm)

SPREAD 4–5in (10–13cm)

SITE Partial shade

SOIL Average, rich in organic matter, free-draining

HARDINESS Z7–9

FLOWERING Mid- and late spring

Cyrtanthus elatus Scarborough lily

YOU NEED A CONSERVATORY to grow this tender South African bulb, which needs to be kept inside over winter, when it is dormant. But stand it outside over summer for end-of-season blooms producing up to nine wonderfully flashy, scarlet flowers. The leaves are like long straps, measuring about 10in (25cm) long. Plant with the bulb's neck at soil level in a pot of loam-based potting mix, with added leaf mold and horticultural sand. Shade from scorching sun. Water freely in full growth and sparingly over winter, when it should be kept at 40–50°F (5–10°C), and add tomato fertilizer in summer. In very mild regions, plant outside at twice the bulb's depth in free-draining soil.

OTHER VARIETY *C. brachyscyphus* (slightly curved red flowers).

PLANT PROFILE

HEIGHT 12–24in (30–60cm)

SPREAD 4in (10cm)

SITE Full sun

SOIL Loam-based potting mix

HARDINESS Z8–10 H10–8

FLOWERING Late summer

D | Dahlia 'Arabian Night'

'ARABIAN NIGHT' HAS DEEP, dark, black-red petals in a round ball, and is equally impressive in the middle of the border and as a cut flower. When three to four pairs of leaves are showing, nip back the stem to create bushier, more flowery plants, and give tomato fertilizer in summer. When frost blackens the leaves, cut back the stems to 6in (15cm) high, dig up the tubers, and remove the soil. Place the tubers upside down to dry, dust with fungicide, and box up in sawdust to overwinter in a cool, frost-free place. Occasionally sprinkle water on the tubers over winter or they might shrivel and die. Also see 'Glorie van Heemstede' (*opposite*).

OTHER VARIETY *D.* 'Edinburgh' (rich purple flowers with a flash of white at the tips of the petals).

PLANT PROFILE
HEIGHT 4ft (1.2m)
SPREAD 24in (60cm)
SITE Full sun
SOIL Fertile
HARDINESS Z8–10
FLOWERING Midsummer, through autumn

Dahlia 'Glorie van Heemstede'

D

A FREE-FLOWERING DAHLIA with rosettes of bright yellow petals held on strong, long stems with upright growth. It is extremely useful in the middle of a border with flashy reds and rich purples. In spring, put the tubers in pots of moist, multipurpose potting mix and keep at 64°F (18°C); three weeks later, new shoots will appear. For prolific flowering, nip back the main stem when three to four pairs of leaves have opened to force out more branches. Stand the pots outside on warm days but bring in at night until there is no danger of frost. Plant out in rich soil in early summer; use stakes to support the branches. See 'Arabian Night' (*opposite*) for more growing tips.

OTHER VARIETY *D.* 'Porcelain' (pure white flowers with a hint of violet-lilac).

PLANT PROFILE	
HEIGHT 4½ft (1.3m)	
SPREAD 24in (60cm)	
SITE Full sun	
SOIL Fertile	
HARDINESS Z8–11 H12–1	
FLOWERING Midsummer to early autumn	

D

Dahlia 'Moonfire'

A TERRIFIC PLANT FOR BORDERS due to its striking combination of dark bronze foliage and open flowers with yellow right in the center, then a ring of red, and a broad band of yellow on the outer half of the petals. Plant *Dahlia* 'Moonfire' with care so that the leaf color makes a lively contrast with adjacent bright greens. Being quite short, it is also suitable for planting in large containers where neighboring plants can be used to support and hold up the branches. See 'Arabian Night' (*page 86*) and 'Glorie van Heemstede' (*page 87*) for growing tips. Dahlias are fun plants that put on a long show of flowers, from mid- or late summer until the first frost.

OTHER VARIETY *D.* 'Ellen Huston' (dark foliage, orange-scarlet flowers).

PLANT PROFILE

HEIGHT 2½–3ft (75–90cm)

SPREAD 18in (45cm)

SITE Full sun

SOIL Fertile

HARDINESS Z7–8

FLOWERING Midsummer to early autumn

Dahlia 'Park Princess'

D

TYPICALLY FOUND IN PUBLIC DISPLAYS, 'Park Princess' is a restrained, pale pink dahlia, in complete contrast to the livelier, punchier kinds, producing swaths of late-summer color. It belongs to a group called the cactus dahlias, with each flower being like a tight ball of outward-pointing petals. Dig it up after the first frost and keep it in a dry, cool, airy place during its dormant winter period. The growing regimen is very easy—see 'Arabian Night' (*page 86*) and 'Glorie van Heemstede' (*page 87*)—but staking is unnecessary because it is short. The only glitch occurs if you don't have suitable winter storage space. Beware of slugs chomping through the stems.

OTHER VARIETY *D.* 'Fascination' (dark bronze foliage, light purple-pink flowers).

PLANT PROFILE
HEIGHT 2–3ft (60–90cm)
SPREAD 18in (45cm)
SITE Full sun
SOIL Fertile
HARDINESS Z8–9
FLOWERING Midsummer to early autumn

D

Dichelostemma ida-maia California firecracker

THIS TERRIFIC NORTH AMERICAN BULB is worth trying for its flowers, like small tubes, that appear at the end of long, thin, wiry stems. They are crimson almost to the tip, where they turn bright green. California firecracker needs a very mild, sunny, sheltered spot when grown outdoors. In autumn, plant the bulbs 4in (10cm) deep in free-draining soil. They like to be kept on the dry side after flowering, which means they are best grown at the foot of a sunny, sheltered wall or in a rock garden. Gravel gardens also provide first-rate drainage.

OTHER VARIETY *D. congestum* (tubular, lilac-blue flowers).

PLANT PROFILE

HEIGHT 8–12in (20–30cm)

SPREAD 2in (5cm)

SITE Full sun

SOIL Free-draining

HARDINESS Z5–8 H8–5

FLOWERING Summer

Eranthis hyemalis Winter aconite

HIGH ON THE LIST of easily grown, must-have bulbs, this winter aconite injects flashy yellow flowers at ankle-height, and is nicely set off by the fresh green ruff of leaves. *Eranthis hyemalis* is great at naturalizing if left alone near shrubs, and looks particularly attractive when it has spread its seed around clumps of hellebores, giving one of the first great sweeps of color after Christmas. Grow winter aconite in borders or wild gardens in damp soil (it must stay damp even in summer) that is rich in organic matter. Plant it 2in (5cm) deep in autumn.

OTHER VARIETY *E. hyemalis* Cilicica Group (bright yellow flowers).

PLANT PROFILE
HEIGHT 2–3in (5–8cm)
SPREAD 2in (5cm)
SITE Full sun or light dappled shade
SOIL Fertile, rich in organic matter, moist
HARDINESS Z4–9 H9–1
FLOWERING Late winter and early spring

E

Erythronium 'Pagoda' Dog's-tooth violet

A BEAUTY OF A NORTH AMERICAN BULB, *Erythronium* 'Pagoda' produces exquisite, sulfur yellow flowers in spring and glossy, deep green leaves with bronze mottling. 'Pagoda' is best grown in moist, shady woodland with plenty of leaf mold, but it will be quite happy planted between border shrubs—just make sure that the flowers can be seen easily. It is important that the soil is kept damp, even during a long, hot summer. Incidentally, the "dog's-tooth" nickname refers to the shape of the bulb and definitely not to the flowers.

OTHER VARIETY *E. dens-canis* (white, pink, or lilac flowers).

PLANT PROFILE
HEIGHT 6–14in (15–35cm)
SPREAD 4in (10cm)
SITE Light or partial shade
SOIL Fertile, rich in organic matter, moist but free-draining
HARDINESS Z4–9 H9–1
FLOWERING Spring

Eucharis amazonica Amazon lily

E

THE AMAZON LILY is an impressive tropical bulb. It has 16in- (40cm-) long, dark green, glossy leaves, and 24in- (60cm-) high, leafless stems with up to eight sweet-scented white flowers at the top. Each flower has six petals around the inner cup. Plant two or three bulbs in a pot in the spring in a loam-based potting mix with added horticultural sand and leaf mold, and place in a conservatory at 70°F (21°C); thereafter, keep it at 65°F (18°C). Over summer, keep the atmosphere humid. Water well in active growth, with a monthly liquid fertilizer. Water sparingly over winter, but never let the soil dry out completely.

PLANT PROFILE

HEIGHT	28in (70cm)
SPREAD	6in (15cm)
SITE	Light dappled shade
SOIL	Loam-based potting mix
HARDINESS	Z14–15 H12–10
FLOWERING	Late summer

E

Eucomis bicolor Pineapple flower

THE TROPICAL-LOOKING FLOWER STEM of *Eucomis bicolor* is encircled by dozens of tiny, pale green-cream, starry flowers with purple margins, on top of which is perched a pineapple-like tuft of leaves. *E. bicolor*, and the spearlike *E. comosa* (*see inset*), used to be thought too tender for the garden, but if you plant them at three times the depth of the bulb, but no deeper than 18in (45cm), they should survive in a sheltered, sunny position, and will gradually build up into large clumps. Alternatively, grow them in pots, keeping them inside over winter. Plant in fertile, free-draining soil and water them regularly over summer.

OTHER VARIETY *E. pallidiflora* (green-white flowers).

PLANT PROFILE

HEIGHT 12–24in (30–60cm)

SPREAD 8in (20cm)

SITE Full sun

SOIL Fertile, free-draining

HARDINESS Z8–10 H10–8

FLOWERING Late summer

Freesia 'Everett'

SOME HARDIER WILD FREESIAS can be grown outdoors, but this is a bright pink beauty for flowering indoors, in the second half of winter. Plant the corms in pots filled with a loam-based potting mix in the autumn, then put in a cool, bright, airy place, keeping the temperature under 55°F (13°C). Provide liquid fertilizer when the buds appear. The temperature can be increased for earlier flowering, but do not let it exceed 60°F (16°C) or the stems will become too spindly. Decrease watering after flowering, and keep dry until next autumn, when they can be started into growth again.

F

PLANT PROFILE

HEIGHT To 16in (40cm)

SITE Full sun

SOIL Loam-based potting mix

HARDINESS Z10–11 H12–6

FLOWERING Late winter

F | *Fritillaria acmopetala* Fritillary

THE LITTLE FLOWERS of *Fritillaria acmopetala* resemble pale green, dangling bells with red-brown chocolate marks on the outside. Found growing in the wild in Turkey, Syria, and Lebanon, they add a gentle, eastern Mediterranean touch to the garden. It is important to provide similar conditions, which means you need to grow *F. acmopetala* in a sunny border or rock garden with excellent drainage and full sun. Alternatively, plant the bulbs at the foot of a sunny wall or in a gravel garden where they will not sit in wet soil while dormant.

PLANT PROFILE

HEIGHT To 16in (40cm)

SPREAD 3in (8cm)

SITE Full sun

SOIL Fertile, free-draining

HARDINESS Z6–8 H8–6

FLOWERING Late spring

Fritillaria biflora 'Martha Roderick' Mission bells

F

THE BELL-SHAPED, DANGLING FLOWERS of *Fritillaria biflora* 'Martha Roderick' appear in clusters of 6–12 on a 10in (25cm), sturdy stem in the first half of spring. The color is basically red-purple with white near the tips. Unlike some of the more popular, widely grown fritillaries, 'Martha Roderick' dislikes damp conditions, which can be fatal. If you cannot provide a free-draining position with adequate shelter from the rain, grow it in pots in a cold greenhouse, and make sure that the soil is kept on the dry side while the bulbs are dormant over summer.

OTHER VARIETY *F. bucharica* (green-veined white flowers).

PLANT PROFILE
HEIGHT 6–12in (15–30cm)
SPREAD 2–3in (5–8cm)
SITE Full sun
SOIL Fertile, free-draining
HARDINESS Z6–9
FLOWERING Early and midspring

F

Fritillaria camschatcensis Black sarana

FOR GARDENERS THINKING OF GOING GOTHIC, *Fritillaria camschatcensis* is a black-purple (though sometimes green or yellow) early summer flower, with up to eight small, bell-like blooms per stem. Each stem can be from 5in (12cm) to over 24in (60cm) high, with whorls of lance-shaped, glossy leaves. In the wild it grows in subalpine meadows and damp woodland, and consequently will not succeed if the planting area has anything other than cool, moist conditions. The soil should also be rich with plenty of leaf mold.

OTHER VARIETY *F. affinis* (green-white flowers with red-purple stains or speckles).

PLANT PROFILE

HEIGHT To 18in (45cm)

SPREAD 3–4in (8–10cm)

SITE Full sun to light shade

SOIL Rich in organic matter, moist with added leaf mold

HARDINESS Z4–9 H8–2

FLOWERING Early summer

Fritillaria imperialis Crown imperial

F

TOTALLY BIZARRE TO LOOK AT, *Fritillaria imperialis* has 3ft- (1m-) high stems, topped with a punkish tuft of upward-pointing leaves and about six red or orange downward-facing flower cups just beneath them. *F. imperialis* 'Maxima Lutea' has yellow flowers (*see inset*). Plant the bulbs around tree trunks or at the back of beds, in tubs or gaps between a row of sculpted boxwood. One by itself looks like an accident, but a group injects panache. Don't be fooled by its exotic looks; it is tougher than you might think, but has an unpleasant foxy scent. Plant the bulbs on their sides to keep water out of the hollow when dormant.

OTHER VARIETY *F. imperialis* 'Lutea' (bright yellow flowers).

PLANT PROFILE	
HEIGHT To 5ft (1.5m)	
SPREAD 10–12in (25–30cm)	
SITE Full sun	
SOIL Fertile, free-draining	
HARDINESS Z5–9 H9–4	
FLOWERING Early summer	

F | *Fritillaria meleagris* Snake's-head fritillary

THE SMALL, LANTERNLIKE FLOWERS of *Fritillaria meleagris* hang down
and are usually intricately checkered purple-pink. Snake's-head
fritillary is typically used to colonize damp, meadowlike grass, where
it has a gentle, unobtrusive presence and is far from being
immediately obvious (the white kind are much more distinctive).
Plant it in drifts about 4in (10cm) deep, and avoid parts of the
garden where the soil bakes dry in summer. If you begin with a
collection of colors, the plants will cross-breed, creating a wider
variety of shades.

OTHER VARIETY *F. meleagris* 'Aphrodite' (large white flowers).

PLANT PROFILE
HEIGHT To 12in (30cm)
SPREAD 2–3in (5–8cm)
SITE Full sun
SOIL Fertile, rich in organic matter, moist but free-draining
HARDINESS Z4–9 H8–2
FLOWERING Spring

Fritillaria pallidiflora Fritillary

F

IT MIGHT NOT BE THAT POPULAR, but *Fritillaria pallidiflora* is incredibly easy to grow, with quite a strong presence, and gentle, creamy yellow, bell-like flowers set against glaucous, gray-green leaves. The best growing location is in fertile, moist soil that does not dry out in summer, so choose a position with light, dappled shade. If clumps become congested, flowering might deteriorate, in which case you should pry the group out of the ground, divide the bulbs, and replant the various sections in other areas, giving them plenty of room to multiply.

PLANT PROFILE
HEIGHT To 16in (40cm)
SPREAD 2–3in (5–8cm)
SITE Full sun or light dappled shade
SOIL Fertile, free-draining
HARDINESS Z4–9 H8–2
FLOWERING Late spring to early summer

F

Fritillaria pudica **Yellow fritillary**

THIS FRITILLARY HAS A REPUTATION for being very tricky, but is well worth trying to grow for its pure yellow flowers. They appear on stems that can reach 8in (20cm) high. Although only a few bulb specialists sell it, the most reliable form is said to be 'Richard Britten', which has larger flowers. Unlike some of the more popular fritillaries, *F. pudica* does not like damp growing conditions, so if you cannot provide free-draining soil with shelter from the rain, grow it in pots in a cold greenhouse, and make sure that it is kept dry when dormant.

PLANT PROFILE

HEIGHT To 8in (20cm)

SPREAD 2in (5cm)

SITE Full sun

SOIL Fertile, free-draining

HARDINESS Z2–9 H9–1

FLOWERING Early spring

Fritillaria uva-vulpis Fritillary

A MINIATURE FRITILLARY with glossy green leaves, *F. uva-vulpis* has bell-shaped, brown-purple flowers with deep yellow tips and covered by a blue–gray hue. In the wild, in Turkey, Iraq, and Iran, it grows in open spaces, but in the garden it requires a location with excellent drainage, which means either a rock or gravel garden. Where it feels at home, it quickly multiplies and creates clumps. It is sometimes still sold as *F. assyriaca*.

PLANT PROFILE
HEIGHT To 8in (20cm)
SPREAD 2in (5cm)
SITE Full sun
SOIL Average, free-draining
HARDINESS Z7–9 H9–1
FLOWERING Spring

OTHER VARIETY *F. tubiformis* (gray-purple flowers, white inside).

G | *Galanthus* 'Atkinsii' Snowdrop

THERE ARE SCORES OF SNOWDROP VARIETIES, though spotting
the difference between some of them sends can be a challenge, even
for the experts. *Galanthus* 'Atkinsii' is typically robust and prolific,
multiplying freely. New bulbs are often sold for planting when still
in leaf (called "in the green"), before going dormant. Although
fairly unfussy about where it's planted, it prefers shade and isn't too
crazy about hot, dry conditions. One of the taller snowdrops,
'Atkinsii' is suitable for cut flower displays. 'Hippolyta', one of the
last snowdrops to flower, is also worth trying.

OTHER VARIETY G. 'Magnet' (large flowers on very long stems).

PLANT PROFILE

HEIGHT 8in (20cm)

SPREAD 3in (8cm)

SITE Partial shade

SOIL Rich in organic matter,
moist but free-draining

HARDINESS Z3–9 H9–1

FLOWERING Late winter

Galanthus elwesii Snowdrop

ANOTHER EXCELLENT SNOWDROP, *Galanthus elwesii* grows in the wild in Turkey in rocky ground. The honey-scented flowers open in late winter, but to get a good whiff you will need to pick them for a cut flower display or get your nose down to the ground. Once a good batch of bulbs have been planted, they will spread to form an attractive clump, perking up the garden before the main spring bulbs take off. Try *G. elwesii* under deciduous trees and shrubs, and also in rock gardens. For growing conditions, see 'Atkinsii' (*opposite*).

OTHER VARIETY *G. nivalis* f. *pleniflorus* 'Flore Pleno' (robust, with irregular double flowers).

PLANT PROFILE
HEIGHT 5–9in (12–22cm)
SPREAD 3in (8cm)
SITE Partial shade
SOIL Rich in organic matter, moist but free-draining
HARDINESS Z3–8H8–1
FLOWERING Late winter

G | *Galanthus nivalis* 'Lady Elphinstone' Common snowdrop

MAKING WONDERFUL SHEETS of white in grass, *Galanthus nivalis* 'Lady Elphinstone' spreads well, and also tends to flower slightly later than most snowdrops. From a distance its distinguishing features are not immediately obvious, but on closer inspection you'll find that, as well as gray-green leaves, it has double white flowers with yellow inner markings. If possible, grow snowdrops against a background of dark green sculpted boxwood to create a striking contrast. See 'Atkinsii' (*page 104*) for growing tips.

OTHER VARIETY *G. nivalis* (honey-scented flowers).

PLANT PROFILE
HEIGHT 5in (12cm)
SPREAD 3in (8cm)
SITE Partial shade
SOIL Rich in organic matter, moist but free-draining
HARDINESS Z3–8 H8–1
FLOWERING Late winter to early spring

Galtonia candicans Summer hyacinth

G

A HIGH-PERFORMANCE, easy-to-spot South African bulb, *Galtonia candicans* has up to 30 slightly scented, tubular flowers, about 2in (5cm) long. The gray-green leaves are long and strap-shaped. Get them off to a good start in spring by planting the bulbs in pots in a conservatory and move them outside at the beginning of summer. They need moist but free-draining soil that will not dry out. In areas with severe winters, lift the bulbs in late autumn, pot them, and keep them in a cool greenhouse until the following year. Alternatively, protect them in the garden with a thick mulch of compost.

PLANT PROFILE		
HEIGHT 3ft (1m)		
SPREAD 4in (10cm)		
SITE Full sun		
SOIL Fertile, moist but free-draining		
HARDINESS Z7–10 H10–7		
FLOWERING Late summer		

G | *Galtonia viridiflora* Green summer hyacinth

THE DANGLING, TRUMPET- or funnel-shaped South African flowers
of *Galtonia viridiflora* are pale green and up to 2in (5cm) long.
Anything from 15 to 30 blooms appear on the strong, upright stems
of each plant. The leaves are broad, dark green, and waxy, and create
a lush look for late summer. Grow as for *G. candicans* (*see page 107*),
and note the importance of planting it in soil that is reasonably
moist over summer, because it must not be allowed to dry out.

PLANT PROFILE
HEIGHT 3ft (1m)
SPREAD 4in (10cm)
SITE Full sun
SOIL Fertile, moist but free-draining
HARDINESS Z8–10 H10–8
FLOWERING Late summer

Gladiolus communis subsp. *byzantinus*

G

A HARDY MEDITERRANEAN GLADIOLUS that does not need any pampering, *G. communis* subsp. *byzantinus* produces bright, brash magenta flowers on top of long stems, giving strong, rich color at about waist-height. It gradually spreads to form large clumps, and puts on a terrific show in the middle of the border. The flowers are good for cutting. Plant the corms in the autumn in free-draining soil where they get a chance to bake over summer. In areas with sharp winter freezes, it benefits from a thick, protective winter mulch.

PLANT PROFILE

HEIGHT To 3ft (1m)

SPREAD 3in (8cm)

SITE Full sun

SOIL Fertile, free-draining

HARDINESS Z8–10 H9–1

FLOWERING Late spring to early summer

G | *Gladiolus* 'Green Woodpecker'

WITH A HIGHLY PRODUCTIVE 25 buds per flower stem, the ruffled blooms of *Gladiolus* 'Green Woodpecker' are an interesting blend of yellow and green, with wine red marks at the throat. 'Green Woodpecker' looks equally good grown next to other scarlet, white, or pastel varieties. If growing gladiolus in a sunny, sheltered site that is frost-free, leave it in the ground over winter. In frosty areas, dig up the bulbs in the autumn, when the leaves turn yellow-brown, and dry for 14 days. Keep in an airy, dry, frost-free place for planting out next spring.

PLANT PROFILE

HEIGHT 5ft (1.5m)

SPREAD 5in (12cm)

SITE Full sun

SOIL Fertile, free-draining

HARDINESS Z8–10 H9–1

FLOWERING Mid- and late summer

Gladiolus 'Nymph'

G

WITH LARGE NUMBERS of brightly colored gladiolus now on the market, it is very useful to have some whites around to provide a lively contrast or embellish groups of pastel colors. The 2in- (5cm-) wide white flowers of *Gladiolus* 'Nymph' actually have creamy white markings edged with red, but they are not in any way gaudy. The need for sun and fast drainage means 'Nymph' can be grown in warm, sheltered gravel gardens and Mediterranean-style designs, where it adds a bright early-summer touch. See 'Green Woodpecker' (*opposite*) for growing tips.

OTHER VARIETY G. 'Charm' (pink flowers with distinctive yellow-green marks).

PLANT PROFILE	
HEIGHT 28in (70cm)	
SPREAD 3–4in (8–10cm)	
SITE Full sun	
SOIL Fertile, free-draining	
HARDINESS Z8–10 H9–1	
FLOWERING Early summer	

G | *Gladiolus papilio*

ORIGINALLY FOUND IN THE WILD in South Africa, *Gladiolus papilio* provides a nice contrast to the archetypal, large-flowering type of gladiolus that garden centers sell by the thousands. It is has small, quirky, bell-shaped flowers varying from bright yellow to yellow-green, heavily marked with purple, on arching stems. The swordlike leaves are up to 18in (45cm) long. If the corms are left alone, they quickly multiply to form large clumps. In frost-prone areas, provide a thick, protective winter mulch or dig them up in the autumn and keep in a container over winter in a frost-free greenhouse.

PLANT PROFILE

HEIGHT 20–36in (50–90cm)

SPREAD 3in (8cm)

SITE Full sun

SOIL Fertile, free-draining

HARDINESS Z8–10 H9–1

FLOWERING Summer to autumn

Gladiolus 'Prins Claus'

G

SOME GLADIOLUS ARE OUT-AND-OUT EXTROVERTS, and 'Prins Claus' is flamboyant enough to be one of them. The petals have large, beautiful red marks or blotches that look like they have been painted on. 'Prins Claus' looks good combined with the kind of strong colors that will not be upstaged—for example the bold, blood red 'Spitfire'—or with quiet pastels whose main function is to provide paler background colors. The flowers of 'Prins Claus' are also good for livening up a cut-flower display. See 'Green Woodpecker' (*page 110*) for growing tips.

PLANT PROFILE	
HEIGHT 28in (70cm)	
SPREAD 3–4in (8–10cm)	
SITE Full sun	
SOIL Fertile, free-draining	
HARDINESS Z8–10 H9–1	
FLOWERING Early summer	

G | *Gladiolus* 'The Bride'

WITH WHITE FLOWERS AND YELLOW MARKINGS, *Gladiolus* 'The Bride' is one of the first gladiolus to break bud in early spring given a hot, sunny spell. When choosing other varieties to complement it, make sure you check their flowering times or you may end up with some that don't bloom until mid– or even late summer, like the vermilion red 'Vaucluse'. The early flowering kind tend to belong to the Nanus Group—which includes 'Amanda Mahy' (salmon pink) and 'Prins Claus' (white with red markings, *page 113*). For tips on how to grow 'The Bride', see 'Green Woodpecker' (*page 110*).

OTHER VARIETY G. 'White City' (taller with white flowers).

PLANT PROFILE

HEIGHT	To 24in (60cm)
SPREAD	2in (5cm)
SITE	Full sun
SOIL	Fertile, free-draining
HARDINESS	Z8–10 H9–1
FLOWERING	Early spring to early summer

Gladiolus tristis

G

THE BEST REASON for growing the wild South African *Gladiolus tristis* is that it has pale yellow or creamy white flowers that are sweetly and strongly scented in the evening. They are usually flushed or speckled in mauve, red, brown, or purple. *G. tristis* also has a much more natural, graceful look, with its funnel-shaped flowers, than the typical gladiolus with strongly colored flowers running up the top of the stem. It is therefore often grown in cottage or informal gardens, where it self-seeds around the borders. See 'Green Woodpecker' (*page 110*) for growing tips.

PLANT PROFILE

HEIGHT 1½–5ft (45–150cm)

SPREAD 2in (5cm)

SITE Full sun

SOIL Ferile, free-draining

HARDINESS Z8–10 H9–1

FLOWERING Spring

H | *Habranthus robustus* Rain lily

THE LONG, PALE PINK FLOWERS of *Habranthus robustus* tend to appear simultaneously with, or just before, the deep green leaves. Originally from Brazil, it needs to be grown in a conservatory, in pots which can be moved outside over summer. Plant the bulbs 3–4in (7–10cm) deep in a loam-based potting mix with added horticultural sand, and water moderately as growth begins, more freely when in leaf. When the buds appear, give a weekly liquid feeding. Reduce watering as the foliage dies, and keep barely moist when dormant.

OTHER VARIETY *H. tubispathus* (copper red, orange, or yellow

PLANT PROFILE	
HEIGHT 8–12in (20–30cm)	
SPREAD 2in (5cm)	
SITE Full sun	
SOIL Fertile, free-draining	
HARDINESS Z7–10 H10–7	
FLOWERING Summer	

Haemanthus coccineus Cape tulip

H

BEGUILING AND SHOWY, the Cape tulip is not what it seems. What looks like one upward-pointing, cup-shaped flower is actually a cluster of up to 100 tiny red blooms locked within the large, scarlet outer "petals." Keep the bulbs in small pots for better flowering. After the flowers, a few leaves up to 18in (45cm) long might appear, and later, fleshy white to pink fruit. Grow bulbs in a loam-based potting mix with added horticultural sand for sharp drainage. Water well in the growing season, and give tomato fertilizer every two weeks. Keep dry when dormant.

OTHER VARIETY *H. albiflos* (tiny white flowers).

PLANT PROFILE
HEIGHT To 14in (35cm)
SPREAD 6in (15cm)
SITE Sun or dappled shade
SOIL Loam-based potting mix
HARDINESS Z13–15 H12–10
FLOWERING Summer to autumn

H | *Hermodactylus tuberosus* Widow iris

A NOVEL CHOICE FOR A MEDITERRANEAN GARDEN, the widow iris
has solitary green-yellow flowers in the spring with velvetlike, black-
brown outer segments. The long leaves have a blue or gray tinge.
Because it comes from rocky areas with hot, dry summers (North
Africa, Israel, and Turkey) it needs to bake through the summer
months, when dormant, if it is to thrive. Make sure that
the site provides excellent drainage—for example, at the base of a
sunny wall, or on sandy or chalky slopes—and plant out in the
autumn, leaving room for it to spread and make clumps. Beware of
slugs and snails attacking the new winter growth.

PLANT PROFILE

HEIGHT 8–16in (20–40cm)

SPREAD 2in (5cm)

SITE Full sun

SOIL Average, free-draining, alkaline

HARDINESS Z7–9 H9–7

FLOWERING Spring

Hippeastrum 'Apple Blossom' Amaryllis

H

OFTEN CALLED AMARYLLIS, hippeastrums make wonderfully showy houseplants. *H.* 'Apple Blossom' has large, white, trumpet-shaped flowers, up to 6in (15cm) wide, with a pink tinge around the edge of the petal tips. Soak the bottom half of the bulb for 24 hours, and then plant in a loam-based potting mix, leaving the top half exposed. Place in bright light and water sparingly; give liquid fertilizer every two weeks when in active growth. After flowering, continue watering, keeping the leaves green for about two months, when they will start to yellow (reduce watering) and die (stop watering). Keep dry for about 12 weeks and then start gently watering again.

OTHER VARIETY *H.* 'White Dazzler' (snow white flowers).

PLANT PROFILE

HEIGHT 12–20in (30–50cm)

SPREAD 12in (30cm)

SITE Sun or dappled shade

SOIL Fertile, free-draining

HARDINESS Z14–15 H12–10

FLOWERING Winter

H

Hyacinthoides hispanica Spanish bluebell

BLUEBELLS ARE IDEAL for bringing spring cheer to a patch of grass in a wild garden or around the base of trees. The Spanish variety is generally considered to be more robust, straighter, and slightly taller than its English relation (*see opposite*). It also flowers all around the stem and is an inveterate invader, multiplying by seed and root, so it is best kept out of a manicured border. Plant the bulbs in large drifts on banks and any spare ground, as long as it is not clay, in light, flickering, woodland-type shade. Do not confuse them with hyacinths, which are totally different.

OTHER VARIETY *H. hispanica* 'Rosabella' (violet-pink flowers).

PLANT PROFILE
HEIGHT 16in (40cm)
SPREAD 4in (10cm)
SITE Dappled shade
SOIL Average, rich in organic matter, moist but free-draining
HARDINESS Z4–10 H9–1
FLOWERING Spring

Hyacinthoides non-scripta English bluebell

H

MAKING ATTRACTIVE CLUMPS of blue flowers, which look like tiny bells on straight stems, the English bluebell adds a lovely woodland touch to gardens. Plant the bulbs in clumps in light shade under trees (especially those with contrasting white trunks), around shrubs, and in areas where wild flowers are allowed to grow. With luck you may be able to track down the white (*see inset*) and pink forms. Avoid heavy clay, and don't confuse them with hyacinths. The Spanish bluebell (*see opposite*) is a good alternative.

OTHER VARIETY *H. hispanica* 'Excelsior' (violet-blue flowers, striped paler blue).

PLANT PROFILE
HEIGHT 8–16in (20–40cm)
SPREAD 3in (8cm)
SITE Dappled shade
SOIL Average, rich in organic matter, moist but free-draining
HARDINESS Z4–10 H9–1
FLOWERING Spring

H | *Hyacinthus orientalis* 'Amethyst' Hyacinth

RICHLY SCENTED, HYACINTHS can be grown as houseplants, but they also make a terrific display in a sunny, sheltered part of the garden, where their perfume hangs in the air. *Hyacinthus orientalis* 'Amethyst' has a particularly strong scent, with scores of tiny flowers typically packed around the flower spike. Group together as many as space allows for maximum impact. Although the number of flowers will decline over the years, the bulbs still put on an impressive show. Plant them in the autumn, 4in (10cm) deep, in average, free-draining soil. Make sure you buy specially prepared bulbs to flower indoors in winter, possibly as early as Christmas.

OTHER VARIETY *H. orientalis* 'Anna Marie' (pale pink flowers).

PLANT PROFILE

HEIGHT 8–12in (20–30cm)

SPREAD 3in (8cm)

SITE Sun or partial shade

SOIL Average, free-draining

HARDINESS Z5–9 H9–5

FLOWERING Early spring

Hyacinthus orientalis 'Blue Jacket' Hyacinth

THE RICH NAVY BLUE, scented flowers of *Hyacinthus orientalis* 'Blue Jacket' have purple veins and make a strong show in front of a white background. 'Blue Jacket' can also be grown with soft yellow hyacinths ('City of Haarlem', *page 125*), pinks ('Lady Derby', *page 126*), and whites ('White Pearl') for a lively combination. As with all richly perfumed hyacinths, it is important to grow the bulbs where they will get plenty of sun in early spring, and in a sheltered part of the garden where their scent will not get blown away. A sunny patio by a back door is ideal. For growing tips, see 'Amethyst' (*opposite*).

OTHER VARIETY *H. orientalis* 'Blue Orchid' (bright blue flowers).

PLANT PROFILE
HEIGHT 8–12in (20–30cm)
SPREAD 3in (8cm)
SITE Sun or partial shade
SOIL Average, free-draining
HARDINESS Z5–9 H9–5
FLOWERING Early spring

H *Hyacinthus orientalis* 'Carnegie' Hyacinth

MAKING AN EXCELLENT CONTRAST to red and blue hyacinths, *H. orientalis* 'Carnegie' gives a compact show of pure white flowers in late spring. Place it in front of a dark background such as a blue fence or wall, or an evergreen shrub like boxwood (*Buxus sempervirens*). Alternatively, use Mexican orange blossom (*Choisya ternata*) to enjoy the added bonus of its powerfully scented white flowers, which open around the same time. 'Carnegie' needs the same growing conditions as 'Amethyst' (*page 122*).

OTHER VARIETY *H. orientalis* 'Ben Nevis' (ivory white flowers).

PLANT PROFILE	
HEIGHT 8–12in (20–30cm)	
SPREAD 3in (8cm)	
SITE Sun or partial shade	
SOIL Average, free-draining	
HARDINESS Z5–9 H9–5	
FLOWERING Late spring	

Hyacinthus orientalis 'City of Haarlem' **Hyacinth**

H

A VERY OLD CULTIVAR, but still a popular choice, *Hyacinthus orientalis* 'City of Haarlem' gives a gentle show of scented yellow flowers in late spring. Its soft color is often contrasted with bolder shades to create a tapestry-like mix—try it with blues ('Blue Jacket'), bright beet-purple ('Distinction'), white ('White Pearl'), and pink ('Lady Derby', *page 126*). Make sure it has a sunny, sheltered site, ideally close to a door or in a window box, where you can be guaranteed to catch its scent. Grow as for 'Amethyst' (*see page 122*).

OTHER VARIETY *H. orientalis* 'Hollyhock' (bright crimson red flowers).

PLANT PROFILE
HEIGHT 8–12in (20–30cm)
SPREAD 3in (8cm)
SITE Sun or partial shade
SOIL Average, free-draining
HARDINESS Z5–9 H9–5
FLOWERING Late spring

H | *Hyacinthus orientalis* 'Lady Derby' Hyacinth

WITH FLOWERS IN A QUIET SHADE of rose pink, 'Lady Derby'
looks highly effective when used as a gentle background to groups
of much more strongly colored hyacinths, and certainly will not
upstage them. It can also be used alone where a low-key planting
is required. Make sure the bulbs are planted in decent numbers in
a sunny, sheltered place where the scent can waft through the
air on bright, hot days. For more advice and growing tips, see
'Amethyst' (*page 122*).

PLANT PROFILE

HEIGHT	8–12in (20–30cm)
SPREAD	3in (8cm)
SITE	Sun or partial shade
SOIL	Average, free-draining
HARDINESS	Z5–9 H9–5
FLOWERING	Early spring

Hyacinthus orientalis 'Ostara' **Hyacinth**

H

GROW 'OSTARA' WITH OTHER HYACINTHS for a mixed color effect, or plant it in a sunny site by the side of a rosemary bush (which shares the same growing conditions) to show off the flowers against the dark green needlelike leaves; prune the rosemary into a stylish geometric shape for an even sharper look. See 'Amethyst' (*page 122*) for tips on cultivation.

OTHER VARIETY *H. orientalis* 'Crystal Palace' (bluebell blue flowers with a touch of white at the edges).

PLANT PROFILE	
HEIGHT 8–12in (20–30cm)	
SPREAD 3in (8cm)	
SITE Sun or partial shade	
SOIL Average, free-draining	
HARDINESS Z5–9 H9–5	
FLOWERING Early spring	

H | *Hyacinthus orientalis* 'Pink Pearl' Hyacinth

IF YOU'RE LOOKING FOR an attractive strong pink, rather than a soft, pastel shade, *Hyacinthus orientalis* 'Pink Pearl' makes a very good choice. It ideally needs a dark-colored background, possibly dark green or blue, to make sure that it really stands out. A site at the base of an evergreen hedge is also well worth trying, particularly in cottage and informal gardens, and should provide enough shelter for the scent to hang in the air. For growing tips, see 'Amethyst' (*page 122*).

OTHER VARIETY *H. orientalis* 'Queen of the Pinks' (deep pink flowers).

PLANT PROFILE
HEIGHT 8–12in (20–30cm)
SPREAD 3in (8cm)
SITE Sun or partial shade
SOIL Average, free-draining
HARDINESS Z5–9 H9–5
FLOWERING Early spring

Hymenocallis x *festalis* Spider lily

THE SIX LONG, THIN, POINTY PETALS of *Hymenocallis* x *festalis* look a little like the legs of a beautiful spider, and surround the central daffodil-like cup. Each bulb produces up to five scented flowers about 5in (12cm) wide, and the leaves reach 3ft (90cm) long, adding to the exotic effect. Plant them in pots in the autumn, leaving the top quarter exposed above the soil, in loam-based potting mix with added horticultural sand. Stand the pots outside during the day over summer, but take them in at night, and apply tomato fertilizer every 14 days. After flowering, allow the growth to die down, and water sparingly over winter. Repot every three to four years.

PLANT PROFILE

HEIGHT 32in (80cm)

SPREAD 12in (30cm)

SITE Sun or partial shade

SOIL Average, moist but free-draining

HARDINESS Z8–10 H10–8

FLOWERING Spring to summer

I

Ipheion 'Rolf Fiedler' Spring starflower

THE VIVID, MID–BLUE, honey-scented flowers of *Ipheion* 'Rolf Fiedler' are outward-facing, star-shaped, and about 1¼in (3cm) wide. You can tell that ipheions are related to the onion family from the strong scent given off by their leaves when crushed. Since 'Rolf Fiedler' is small and slightly tender, it needs to be grown in rock gardens in a sunny, sheltered site, where it soon forms decent clumps. Plant the bulbs at the start of autumn in free-draining soil. In cold regions, a thick, protective winter mulch might help.

PLANT PROFILE

HEIGHT 4–5in (10–12cm)

SITE Full sun

SOIL Average, rich in organic matter, moist but free-draining

HARDINESS Z6–9 H9–6

FLOWERING Spring

Ipheion uniflorum 'Froyle Mill' Spring starflower

I

VIGOROUS AND CLUMP FORMING, *Ipheion uniflorum* 'Froyle Mill' produces upward-facing, star-shaped, scented flowers in a dusky violet color. It multiplies quickly, and puts on a good show in the spring between shrubs, in front of peonies and hostas, or at the edge of a rock garden where it can be clearly seen. The strap-shaped, 10in- (25cm-) long leaves appear in late autumn, and have a bluish tinge. Clumps can be dug up and separated in the autumn—each piece must have a good root system to create new plants—but if left untouched, large drifts make a fine sight. Grow as for 'Rolf Fiedler' (*see opposite*).

OTHER VARIETY *I. uniflorum* 'Album' (pure white flowers).

PLANT PROFILE
HEIGHT 6–8in (15–20cm)
SITE Full sun
SOIL Average, rich in organic matter, moist but free-draining
HARDINESS Z6–9 H9–6
FLOWERING Spring

I *Ipheion uniflorum* 'Wisley Blue' **Spring starflower**

SIMILAR TO *Ipheion uniflorum* 'Froyle Mill' (*see page 131*), lilac-blue-flowered 'Wisley Blue' is the one to choose if you need a slightly stronger color, though the two can be mixed to make an attractive group. 'Wisley Blue' can also be grown in front of peonies and hostas, in rock gardens, and between shrubs. As with all ipheions, beware of slugs and snails, which can be a major nuisance in the spring when the succulent flowering stems start to appear. See 'Rolf Fiedler' (*page 130*) for growing tips.

PLANT PROFILE

HEIGHT 6–8in (15–20cm)

SITE Full sun

SOIL Average, rich in organic matter, moist but free-draining

HARDINESS Z6–9 H9–6

FLOWERING Spring

Iris aucheri

I

STOCKY, ROBUST, AND BEAUTIFUL, *Iris aucheri* has two or three
light blue (*see inset*) to dark blue, violet, or white flowers, measuring
about 2½in (6cm) wide. In the wild, it grows in Iraq and Iran, and it
therefore needs similar garden conditions, with excellent drainage in
a sheltered hot spot, and a chance to bake over summer. Rockeries
are ideal, partly because the small plant is raised up, making it much
more visible than it is down at ground level. Alternatively, grow
I. aucheri toward the front of a gravel or Mediterranean garden. It is
sometimes listed under the Juno irises in specialist bulb catalogs.

OTHER VARIETY *I. cycloglossa* (taller, with pale violet flowers).

PLANT PROFILE

HEIGHT 4–8in (10–20cm)

SITE Full sun

SOIL Free-draining, neutral
or slightly alkaline

HARDINESS Z3–9 H9–1

FLOWERING Late winter or
spring

Iris bucharica

A VIGOROUS BULB, the flowers of *Iris bucharica* are either golden yellow or a combination of white with yellow, and the leaves are glossy green. Like *I. aucheri* (*see page 133*), this native of northeast Afghanistan needs excellent drainage in a sheltered garden hot spot, and a chance to bake over summer. It is an ideal choice for rock, gravel, or Mediterranean-style gardens, or a position at the foot of a sunny wall. It is sometimes listed under the Juno irises in bulb catalogs; some are hard to grow, but *I. bucharica* is the easiest.

OTHER VARIETY *I. magnifica* (*see page 145*).

PLANT PROFILE

HEIGHT 8–16in (20–40cm)

SITE Full sun

SOIL Free-draining, neutral or slightly alkaline

HARDINESS Z5–9 H9–5

FLOWERING Spring

Iris 'Cantab'

I

A FLASH OF YELLOW on the outer pale blue petals of *Iris* 'Cantab' adds a gentle, colorful touch at the end of winter. It belongs to a hardy group called the Reticulata irises, which need free-draining soil so that they get a chance to bake over summer when dormant. This regimen, and the fact that the plants are so small, means that they are best grown in rock or gravel gardens where they are more visible. You can also grow them in pots, which can be brought inside and placed on a sunny windowsill when the plants flower.

OTHER VARIETY *I.* 'Edward' (dark blue flowers with orange marks).

PLANT PROFILE
HEIGHT 4–6in (10–15cm)
SPREAD 1–2in (2.5–5cm)
SITE Full sun
SOIL Fertile, free-draining, neutral to slightly alkaline
HARDINESS Z5–8 H8–5
FLOWERING Late winter and early spring

I

Iris 'Clairette'

DELIGHTFULLY TINY, *Iris* 'Clairette' has pale blue flowers with a deep violet mark that appear right at the end of winter. Similar to 'Cantab' (*see page 135*), it is also a Reticulata iris and needs the same growing conditions. They include raised beds filled with free-draining soil (with plenty of added horticultural sand) in full sun, and small ornamental pots for courtyards and patios. The advantage of using pots is that they can be kept under shelter and on the dry side over summer, because too much rain while the bulbs are dormant can be fatal.

OTHER VARIETY *I. histrioides* (dark blue flowers with deeper blue spotting and a yellow central ridge).

PLANT PROFILE

HEIGHT 4in (10cm)

SITE Full sun

SOIL Free-draining, neutral or slightly alkaline

HARDINESS Z5–9 H8–4

FLOWERING Late winter

Iris danfordiae

I

THE ATTRACTIVE YELLOW FLOWERS of *Iris danfordiae* have green speckling in the middle, and make a pretty show in rock and gravel gardens. Like 'Cantab' (*see page 135*), it is a Reticulata iris and needs the same conditions, with one proviso: if you want the bulbs to increase in number, you must plant them quite deep, anywhere from 4 to 8in (10 to 20cm); if you don't, the very small "baby" bulbs that soon appear will take years to reach flowering size. It is also a good idea to give them liquid tomato fertilizer in midwinter to boost their flowering potential.

OTHER VARIETY *I.* 'Jeannine' (violet flowers with an orange mark, lightly scented).

PLANT PROFILE
HEIGHT 3–6in (8–15cm)
SPREAD 2in (5cm)
SITE Full sun
SOIL Free-draining, neutral or slightly alkaline
HARDINESS Z5–8 H8–4
FLOWERING Late winter and early spring

I

Iris 'Frank Elder'

IN LATE WINTER, *Iris* 'Frank Elder' provides a mix of blue and yellow-green sturdy flowers. Similar to 'Cantab' (*see page 135*), it is also a Reticulata iris and needs the same conditions, with an emphasis on fast drainage and plenty of summer sun. For that reason, pots and containers are a good choice, enabling you to provide the right conditions and move the bulbs into the foreground when the plants start flowering. Alternatively, give 'Frank Elder' a prominent position in a raised bed or gravel garden, or at the foot of a sunny wall.

OTHER VARIETY *I.* 'Hercules' (rich purple petals with orange marks).

PLANT PROFILE
HEIGHT 6in (15cm)
SITE Full sun
SOIL Free-draining, neutral or slightly alkaline
HARDINESS Z3–9 H9–1
FLOWERING Late winter

Iris 'George'

I

THE RICH PURPLE FLOWERS of *Iris* 'George' appear right at the start of spring. 'George' is a well-balanced and sturdy Reticulata iris and needs the same growing conditions as 'Cantab' (*see page 135*). Grow it against a white or green background such as a group of trees with striking white trunks or an evergreen shrub, or around the base of a standard bay tree in a pot for a sharp color contrast.

PLANT PROFILE

HEIGHT	5in (12cm)
SITE	Full sun
SOIL	Free-draining, neutral or slightly alkaline
HARDINESS	Z5–8 H8–5
FLOWERING	Early spring

OTHER VARIETY *I.* 'J. S. Dijt' (red-purple flowers).

I

Iris 'Harmony'

RICH BLUE IS A LOVELY COLOR to have in the garden right at the end of winter when it is rarely seen and, as an added attraction, the petals of *Iris* 'Harmony' also have a yellow flash. Like 'Cantab' (*see page 135*), this Reticulata iris needs good sun and free drainage. Grow it with the white 'Natasha' and the purple 'Pauline' for a lively combination, making sure that they are right at the front of a raised bed or gravel garden where they can be easily seen. 'Harmony' can also be used as a color contrast to a group of early flowering *Narcissus* 'Peeping Tom' and *N. cyclamineus* (*see page 210*), though in chilly weather the daffodils might appear after the irises.

PLANT PROFILE	
HEIGHT 4–6in (10–15cm)	
SPREAD 1–2in (2.5–5cm)	
SITE Full sun	
SOIL Free-draining, neutral or slightly alkaline	
HARDINESS Z5–8 H8–5	
FLOWERING Late winter	

Iris histrioides 'Major'

I

VIGOROUS AND A VERY GOOD CHOICE for cool-climate gardens, *Iris histrioides* 'Major' is perfectly hardy and flowers in early spring, even when the frosts are still striking. A good alternative is 'George' (*see page 139*), which has slightly larger purple flowers. This Reticulata iris needs the same conditions as 'Cantab' (*see page 135*). Its small size means it needs to be placed where it can be clearly seen, one good option being a container that can be moved to a more prominent position when the flowers start to appear.

OTHER VARIETY *I.* 'Gordon' (bright blue flowers with orange marks).

PLANT PROFILE	
HEIGHT 4–6in (10–15cm)	
SPREAD 2–3in (5–7cm)	
SITE Full sun	
SOIL Free-draining, neutral or slightly alkaline	
HARDINESS Z5–8 H8–4	
FLOWERING Early spring	

I

Iris 'Joyce'

IF YOU WANT TO HAVE A SEQUENCE of the small Reticulata irises, many of which start flowering in late winter, 'Joyce' is the one to end with because it blooms at the start of spring. The very attractive flowers are deep sky blue with a yellow flash in the center, and show up well against a background of evergreen leaves. It can also be used to contrast with the early daffodils and tulips that start to open at the same time. Like 'Cantab' (*see page 135*), it needs good drainage and plenty of summer sun when it is dormant.

OTHER VARIETY *I. histrioides* 'Lady Beatrice Stanley' (pale blue flowers).

PLANT PROFILE
HEIGHT 5in (12cm)
SPREAD 2–3in (5–7cm)
SITE Full sun
SOIL Free-draining, neutral or slightly alkaline
HARDINESS Z5–9 H8–4
FLOWERING Early spring

Iris 'Katharine Hodgkin'

I

A VIGOROUS IRIS FOR LATE WINTER, 'Katharine Hodgkin' has delicately patterned blue flowers with yellow and blue marks. With luck, it will soon create decent clumps that you can dig up and divide in the autumn; provided they have roots, replant the sections around the garden. It can be grown to contrast with the very first daffodils, though in cold spells the latter might not open for a few more weeks. This Reticulata iris needs the same conditions as 'Cantab' (*see page 135*). Make sure it is planted where it can be clearly seen.

OTHER VARIETY *I.* 'Gordon' (bright blue flowers, petals are darker with an orange mark).

PLANT PROFILE
HEIGHT 5in (12cm)
SPREAD 2–3in (5–7cm)
SITE Full sun
SOIL Free-draining, neutral or slightly alkaline
HARDINESS Z5–9 H8–4
FLOWERING Late winter

I

Iris latifolia English iris

OPENING IN SHADES OF BLUE, white, and yellow, the flowers of *Iris latifolia* emerge at the top of stems up to 24in (60cm) high. Unlike the other irises listed in this book, it is quite happy growing in clumps of grass; just give it space in moist but free-draining soil. Try it around apple trees in cottage gardens and on sunny slopes. Despite being called the English iris, it is actually 100 percent Spanish and comes from the Pyrenees.

OTHER VARIETY *I. latifolia* 'Duchess of York' (purple flowers).

PLANT PROFILE

HEIGHT 10–24in (25–60cm)

SITE Full sun

SOIL Moist but free-draining, neutral or slightly alkaline

HARDINESS Z5–8 H8–5

FLOWERING Early summer

Iris magnifica

FOUND GROWING ON STEEP, rocky slopes in central Asia, *Iris magnifica* can have as many as 16 arching, glossy leaves about 7in (18cm) long, and up to seven flowers in the second half of spring. They are pale lilac with a yellow and white marking. Make sure that the soil is free-draining, and the site is warm and sunny. Given these conditions—for example, in a gravel or Mediterranean-style garden—a few initial bulbs will eventually produce a showy clump.

OTHER VARIETY *I. aucheri* (*see page 133*).

PLANT PROFILE
HEIGHT 12–24in (30–60cm)
SITE Full sun
SOIL Free-draining
HARDINESS Z6–8 H8–6
FLOWERING Mid- and late spring

I

Iris 'Natascha'

THE FLOWERS of *Iris* 'Natascha' are such a pale blue that they actually appear gray-white in full sun, and only have a bluish tinge at dawn and dusk when the light levels change, and on cloudy days. They appear in early spring, and add a gentle touch with a bit more elegance and style than many other bulbs (for example, some daffodils) at this time. Being very small, 'Natascha' needs to be positioned right at the front of a display so it can be clearly seen. See 'Cantab' (*page 135*) for growing conditions.

PLANT PROFILE

HEIGHT 5in (12cm)

SITE Full sun

SOIL Free-draining, neutral or slightly alkaline

HARDINESS Z5–8 H8–5

FLOWERING Early spring

Iris 'Pauline'

I

FOR THOSE WHO LOVE REALLY DARK IRISES, 'Pauline' is a beautiful dark purple with deep purple markings and a white center. At just 5in (12cm) high, it needs to be planted in rock gardens, windowboxes, or pots, or right at the front of a bed where it can be clearly seen. 'Pauline' is also suitable for growing in specially created spaces between patio paving. Similar to 'Cantab' (*see page 135*), it is also a Reticulata iris, and needs the same conditions.

PLANT PROFILE

HEIGHT 5in (12cm)

SITE Full sun

SOIL Free-draining, neutral or slightly alkaline

HARDINESS Z5–8 H8–5

FLOWERING Early spring

I

Iris 'Professor Blaauw'

AMONG THE LAST OF THE IRISES TO FLOWER, violet-blue 'Professor Blaauw' may still be in bloom on the verge of midsummer. With its yellow-marked petals, it puts on a gentle show in borders and where a touch of stylish elegance is required, such as in Japanese-style gardens. Or try growing it next to statues or large urns and pots to embellish the display. Free-draining soil and a sunny position are vital.

PLANT PROFILE

HEIGHT To 24in (60cm)

SITE Full sun

SOIL Free-draining, neutral or slightly alkaline

HARDINESS Z3–9 H9–1

FLOWERING Midspring to midsummer

Iris reticulata Netted iris

I

A GOOD WAY OF ENLIVENING ROCK GARDENS at the end of winter is by using *Iris reticulata*, which gets just above ankle-high. The color varies from pale to deep violet-blue (*see inset*), or even red-purple, with a yellow mark. When it is happy in free-draining soil in full sun, it creates good-sized clumps. It can also be grown right at the front of borders, in gravel and Mediterranean-style gardens, as well as in pots and windowboxes. Similar to 'Cantab' (*see page 135*), it thrives in the same conditions.

OTHER VARIETY *I.* 'Purple Gem' (neat purple flowers).

PLANT PROFILE
HEIGHT 4–6in (10–15cm)
SITE Full sun
SOIL Free-draining, neutral or slightly alkaline
HARDINESS Z5–9 H8–4
FLOWERING Late winter and early spring

I

Iris winogradowii

A NATIVE OF THE CAUCASUS, this tiny, beautiful iris has pale primrose yellow flowers, measuring about 3in (7cm) wide, which open in early spring. The leaves develop after the flowers. Make sure *Iris winogradowii* is planted in small clusters, and right at the front of the site, so that it can be clearly seen. It likes a slightly cool, moist position with free-draining soil where it will not bake dry over summer, so don't be tempted to put it in a sunny rock garden.

PLANT PROFILE

HEIGHT 2¼–4in (6–10cm)

SITE Full sun

SOIL Moist but free-draining, neutral or slightly alkaline

HARDINESS Z6–8 H8–6

FLOWERING Early spring

Iris xiphium Spanish iris

I

THE PALE TO DEEP BLUE OR VIOLET FLOWERS of *Iris xiphium* appear in pairs at the start of summer. Its 5in- (12cm-) wide flowers are sometimes even yellow or white (*see inset*), and the petals are marked with orange or yellow. At something like 24in (60cm) high, it makes an attractive show with the leaves appearing in the autumn and lasting over winter. The Spanish iris is not particularly fussy, and thrives in full sun on free-draining soil. In the wild it grows in a wide range of habitats.

PLANT PROFILE

HEIGHT 16–24in (40–60cm)

SITE Full sun

SOIL Free-draining, neutral or slightly alkaline

HARDINESS Z5–9 H9–5

FLOWERING Late spring and early summer

I

Ixia paniculata Corn lily

THE 5–18 BISCUIT YELLOW FLOWERS produced on each stem are shaped like open stars, and have a tinge of pink. The corn lily is best grown in a very sheltered, sunny, frost-free site, such as at the foot of a wall where there is free-draining soil. Mulch to provide winter protection. Alternatively, grow it in a pot filled with a loam-based potting mix, planting the bulbs 4–6in (10–15cm) deep. Water sparingly until the flower spike appears, then water freely and give tomato fertilizer every two to three weeks until the foliage starts to die. Keep dry over winter while dormant.

OTHER VARIETY *I. monadelpha* (white, blue, purple, or pink flowers).

PLANT PROFILE

HEIGHT 12–36in (30–90cm)

SITE Full sun

SOIL Average, free-draining

HARDINESS Z10–11

FLOWERING Spring to early summer

Ixia viridiflora Corn lily

I

THIS HIGHLY RATED SOUTH AFRICAN PLANT is well worth growing for its attractive, starlike flowers, which are pale blue-green with a red-rimmed black center. The flowers appear one above the other on the top half of the wiry stems. It is best grown in a cool greenhouse. Plant the corms in autumn 4–6in (10–15cm) deep and 2–3in (5–8cm) apart in pots, adding sharp sand to improve the drainage. Water sparingly until the flower stems appear, then water freely with liquid tomato fertilizer every two to three weeks until the foliage begins to die. Keep dry and frost-free while dormant.

PLANT PROFILE

HEIGHT 12–24in (30–60cm)

SITE Full sun

SOIL Loam-based potting mix

HARDINESS Z10–11 H12–7

FLOWERING Spring to early summer

I | *Ixiolirion tataricum* Siberian lily

HARDLY EVER SEEN because it can be tricky to grow, *Ixiolirion tataricum* is the perfect plant if you're after something unusual. It produces clusters of up to ten funnel-shaped, blue or violet-blue flowers, with a dark central stripe on each petal, so it is well worth a try. You need free-draining soil, and a site where it can bake over summer, sheltered from rain—the base of a sunny wall, for example. Alternatively, grow in a pot filled with a loam-based potting mix. Water freely when in growth, keeping it just moist in autumn and winter; it needs to be kept dry when dormant in late summer.

PLANT PROFILE

HEIGHT 10–16in (24–40cm)

SPREAD 2in (5cm)

SITE Full sun

SOIL Fertile, free-draining

HARDINESS Z10–11 H12–7

FLOWERING Spring to early summer

Lachenalia aloides 'Nelsonii' Cape cowslip

L

UNLESS YOU HAVE A MILD, FROST-FREE GARDEN, you will need to grow this flashy, yellow South African bulb in a conservatory. It has clusters of distinctive, waxy, tubular to bell-shaped flowers, turning scarlet at the tips. The leaves, verging on the fleshy succulent, are blotched and mottled with dark marks. Plant bulbs 4in (10cm) deep in pots filled with a loam-based potting mix. Water moderately until in full growth, then water freely, adding liquid fertilizer every 10–14 days. Reduce watering as the leaves fade, then keep dry until fresh growth starts in autumn.

OTHER VARIETY *L. aloides* 'Pearsonii' (apricot flowers).

PLANT PROFILE

HEIGHT 6–11in (15–28cm)

SPREAD 2in (5cm)

SITE Full light

SOIL Light, free-draining

HARDINESS Z12–14 H12–6

FLOWERING Winter or early spring

L *Leucocoryne ixioides* Glory of the sun

THIS VERY UNDERRATED SOUTH AMERICAN BULB has small, scented, white or lilac-blue flowers; the white ones have purple veins, and the lilac-blue have white throats. The grasslike leaves grow up to 18in (45cm) long and smell of garlic. Plant the bulbs 4in (10cm) deep in pots filled with a loam-based potting mix with added horticultural sand. Water moderately in growth, and apply liquid fertilizer monthly when the leaves appear. Reduce the watering after flowering, and keep almost dry when dormant in summer. Move into a larger pot every two years, in autumn.

OTHER VARIETY *L. purpurea* (scented, pale lilac flowers).

PLANT PROFILE
HEIGHT 18in (45cm)
SPREAD 3in (8cm)
SITE Full sun
SOIL Loam-based potting mix
HARDINESS Z12–14 H8–1
FLOWERING Spring

Leucojum aestivum 'Gravetye Giant' Summer snowflake

L

IMPRESSIVELY ROBUST, VIGOROUS, AND TALL, *Leucojum aestivum* 'Gravetye Giant' sends up leafless stems with as many as eight white, dangling, green-tipped bells, with just the faintest hint of a chocolate scent. If it is to have any impact in the garden, it must be grown in the rich, moist soil that it needs to thrive, making it a good choice for a wild garden, by a stream or natural pond. It is a better bet than its parent, *L. aestivum*, which is not quite as tall. The name "summer snowflake" is completely misleading because it actually flowers in the second half of spring.

PLANT PROFILE	
HEIGHT 3ft (1m)	
SITE Full sun	
SOIL Fertile, moist	
HARDINESS Z3–8 H8–1	
FLOWERING Spring	

L

Leucojum autumnale Autumn snowflake

MUCH SMALLER THAN THE summer snowflake (*Leucojum aestivum*), *L. autumnale* grows ankle-high and has incredibly thin, grasslike, dark green leaves, measuring about 6in (16cm) long. They appear with or just after the white flowers, of which there are two to four. Free-draining or sandy soil is best, because it comes from hot, stony sites around the Mediterranean; given similar garden conditions, it will soon make beautiful clumps. *L. autumnale* is a good choice for rock and gravel gardens or dry slopes and banks, all of which have excellent drainage. Failing that, try the foot of a sunny wall.

PLANT PROFILE

HEIGHT 4–6in (10–15cm)

SPREAD 2in (5cm)

SITE Full sun

SOIL Moist, free-draining

HARDINESS Z5–9 H9–1

FLOWERING Late summer and early autumn

Leucojum vernum Spring snowflake

 L

THE SPRING SNOWFLAKE is a small, robust plant with bell-shaped, green-tipped white flowers—just one appearing on each stem. It makes a good choice if you want something a bit larger than snowdrops in early spring, and has glossy, dark green leaves that grow up to 10in (25cm) long. To thrive, *Leucojum vernum* needs a site with damp, rich soil, and is often grown in short, not-too-vigorous competing grass, where it makes attractive clumps. It even looks good in bad weather and does not sulk. After flowering, clumps can be dug up, divided, and replanted around the garden while they are still in leaf.

OTHER VARIETY *L. vernum* var. *carpathicum* (yellow-tipped petals).

PLANT PROFILE	
HEIGHT 8–12in (20–30cm)	
SPREAD 3in (8cm)	
SITE Full sun	
SOIL Fertile, moist	
HARDINESS Z4–8 H8–1	
FLOWERING Early spring	

L   *Lilium* 'African Queen' Lily

THE FLARED, TRUMPET-SHAPED, and scented flowers of *Lilium* 'African Queen' are brown-purple outside and yellow or apricot orange within. It tolerates most soils but does best on free-draining ground enriched with leaf mold or well-rotted organic matter. Plant at twice the depth of the bulb on heavy soil, or three times the depth of the bulb on light soil. The flowers like sun, and the stem bases like shade. To ward off slugs, cover the surrounding area with sand, use beer traps to lure them away, or grow the bulbs in pots, topping the potting mix with sand. Water well in dry summer spells, and promptly remove any small, bright red lily beetles.

OTHER VARIETY *L.* 'Black Dragon' (flowers are dark purple-red outside, white inside).

PLANT PROFILE

HEIGHT 5–6ft (1.5–2m)

SITE Full sun

SOIL Fertile, free-draining

HARDINESS Z3–8 H8–1

FLOWERING Mid- and late summer

Lilium 'Apollo' Lily

L

A DWARF LILY SUITABLE FOR CONTAINERS, the creamy white flowers of 'Apollo' are also good for cutting. Use a good, loam-based potting mix in deep pots, with added horticultural sand to facilitate drainage. Water freely when in full growth, and apply tomato fertilizer every two weeks. Keep moist over winter, but not soaking wet. If you intend to plant it in borders, see 'African Queen' (*opposite*) for growing tips.

PLANT PROFILE	
HEIGHT 4ft (1.2m)	
SITE Full sun	
SOIL Fertile, free-draining	
HARDINESS Z3–8 H8–1	
FLOWERING Midsummer	

OTHER VARIETY *L.* 'Butter Pixie' (bright butter yellow flowers).

L

Lilium 'Black Beauty' Lily

'BLACK BEAUTY' HAS STARTLING black-red flowers with a green starlike shape in the center. The petals bend and curve back so that they almost touch behind the flower's head, in what gardening books call a turkscap shape. It makes a lively contrast planted next to white hollyhocks (*Alcea rosea*) that tower high above it, or with adjacent dashes of bright red and yellow. 'Black Beauty' is sometimes listed under the Species Hybrids in bulb catalogs. For more information and growing tips, see 'African Queen' (*page 160*).

PLANT PROFILE

HEIGHT	4½–6ft (1.4–2m)
SITE	Full sun
SOIL	Fertile, free-draining
HARDINESS	Z3–8 H8–1
FLOWERING	Midsummer

Lilium 'Bright Star' **Lily**

AN EYE-CATCHING LILY for mid- and late summer, 'Bright Star' has white, trumpet-shaped flowers curving back at the tips, and the petals are imprinted with an orange, starlike shape. It is a good choice if you need a contrast with vibrant red or richly colored lilies, or for filling out an all-white plan with an extra dash of color. Use it in formal garden or cottage gardens, and in large tubs with an extravagant show of fuchsias, daturas, and passionflowers. It needs the same conditions as 'African Queen' (*see page 160*) but also tolerates alkaline soil.

OTHER VARIETY *L.* Olympic Group (flowers are green-white, white, cream, and yellow, to pink and purple, often with yellow throats).

PLANT PROFILE	
HEIGHT 3–5ft (1–1.5m)	
SITE Full sun	
SOIL Fertile, free-draining	
HARDINESS Z3–8 H8–1	
FLOWERING Mid- and late summer	

L

Lilium canadense Meadow lily

THE MEADOW LILY IS AN EXCELLENT CHOICE for dappled shade, where its yellow flowers brighten things up, and it produces whorls of 6in– (15cm–) long leaves, each with parallel veins. In midsummer there are up to ten lightly scented, almost trumpet-shaped, graceful blooms, usually with an attractive scattering of maroon spots in the middle; the tips of the petals curve back. It enjoys a position in moist ground. For growing tips, see 'African Queen' (*page 160*).

OTHER VARIETY *L. canadense* var. *coccineum* (bright red flowers with yellow throats).

PLANT PROFILE

HEIGHT 3–5½ft (1–1.6m)

SITE Dappled shade

SOIL Fertile, free-draining

HARDINESS Z2–6 H6–1

FLOWERING Mid- and late summer

Lilium candidum Madonna lily

L

THE WHITE MADONNA LILY dates back to the time of the ancient Greeks, and is a first-rate, sweetly scented plant. Up to 15 2½in- (6.5cm-) wide, trumpet-shaped flowers emerge on top of a stem with many small leaves lower down. There are also ground-level leaves over winter. Plant the bulbs in the autumn with their tips just beneath the surface, about ¾in (2cm) deep, in average to fertile, free-draining soil. It tolerates slightly drier soils than most lilies, but otherwise grow as for 'African Queen' (*see page 160*).

OTHER VARIETY *L. cernuum* (pale lilac, pink, or purple flowers).

PLANT PROFILE

HEIGHT 3–6ft (1–1.8m)

SITE Full sun

SOIL Fertile, free-draining

HARDINESS Z6–9 H9–6

FLOWERING Midsummer

L

Lilium 'Casa Blanca' Lily

THIS LILY HAS AN EXCELLENT REPUTATION for its clusters of large, pure white, sweetly scented flowers on top of thick, stiff stems; the petal tips curve backward. 'Casa Blanca' makes a strong garden show, and needs a dark green or dark-colored background to stand out well. It excels in all kinds of garden designs, but looks especially good in one with an informal, cottage-garden touch. It is often listed as an Oriental Hybrid in bulb catalogs. For growing tips, see 'African Queen' (*page 160*).

OTHER VARIETY *L. auratum* var. *virginale* (white with yellow streaks and yellow or pink spots).

PLANT PROFILE

HEIGHT 3–4ft (1–1.2m)

SITE Full sun

SOIL Fertile, free-draining

HARDINESS Z3–8 H8–1

FLOWERING Mid- and late summer

Lilium 'Citronella' Lily

A FIRM FAVORITE, *Lilium* 'Citronella' has upright stems with dangling, downward-facing, bright yellow to lemon yellow flowers with faint reddish speckling inside, and petal tips that curve back. From a distance, the flowers look like large, exotic butterflies hovering in the air. 'Citronella' can also be grown in large pots with other plants, shooting up out of the greenery at the bottom to add a colorful aerial touch. Grow as for 'African Queen' (*see page 160*).

OTHER VARIETY *L.* 'Ariadne' (pale orange flowers with purple tips).

PLANT PROFILE	
HEIGHT 4–5ft (1.2–1.5m)	
SITE Full sun	
SOIL Fertile, free-draining	
HARDINESS Z3–8	
FLOWERING Midsummer	

L

Lilium 'Connecticut King' Lily

THE RICH, DEEP YELLOW FLOWERS of *Lilium* 'Connecticut King' make a bright, long-lasting show; the petals curve back slightly at the tips and have an eye-catching, upward-facing star shape. On the short side for a lily, it can be grown toward the front of a border, where it has plenty of presence. Smaller lilies like this can also be used to encircle standard roses and evergreens, such as bay laurel (*Laurus nobilis*). For growing tips, see 'African Queen' (*page 160*).

OTHER VARIETY *L.* 'Chinook' (pale apricot-buff flowers).

PLANT PROFILE

HEIGHT 3ft (1m)

SITE Full sun

SOIL Fertile, free-draining

HARDINESS Z3–8 H8–1

FLOWERING Early and midsummer

Lilium duchartrei Marble martagon lily

L

A VERY BEAUTIFUL WHITE LILY from the mountains of western China, the scented *Lilium duchartrei* has approximately 12 nodding flowers on wiry stems and swept-back petals with purple spots and streaks. The white gradually turns purple-red on the outside. In time, creeping underground sections produce new bulbs, about 12in (30cm) away from the parent, creating impressive colonies. For that reason, leave some room for the bulbs to spread. A semishady, cool position with added leaf mold is ideal, but otherwise grow as for 'African Queen' (*see page 160*).

OTHER VARIETY *L. taliense* (white flowers with purple spots within).

PLANT PROFILE

HEIGHT 24–39in
(60–100cm)

SITE Light shade

SOIL Fertile, free-draining

HARDINESS Z7–8 H8–7

FLOWERING Summer

L

Lilium 'Enchantment' Lily

A VIGOROUS BULB, *Lilium* 'Enchantment' soon creates impressive clumps of cup-shaped, vibrant orange flowers with black spots and fresh green leaves. Use it in brightly colored hothouse or subtropical borders, where flashy, vivid colors are required among plants that reliably produce large, flamboyant, architectural leaves. Introduced in 1947, 'Enchantment' is still going strong and makes good cut flowers. Grow as for 'African Queen' (*see page 160*).

OTHER VARIETY *L*. 'Festival' (pale orange with a deep red central star, brown spots and red tips and margins, often flushed purple-brown).

PLANT PROFILE

HEIGHT 24–39in (60–100cm)

SITE Full sun

SOIL Fertile, free-draining

HARDINESS Z2–8 H8–1

FLOWERING Early summer

Lilium 'Fire King' Lily

L

IDEAL FOR HOTHOUSE OR SUBTROPICAL BORDERS, and those
with "in-your-face" color schemes that disdain subtlety and
immediately grab the eye, the vigorous *Lilium* 'Fire King' has
bright orange flowers with purple spots inside; the tips of the
petals curve back slightly. It is also excellent in a large container,
particularly one with a group of white or pastel-colored flowers,
where it adds a dashing highlight. 'Fire King' is as popular now as
when it was first introduced in the 1930s. For growing tips, see
'African Queen' (*page 160*).

PLANT PROFILE

HEIGHT 3–4ft (1–1.2m)

SITE Full sun

SOIL Fertile, free-draining

HARDINESS Z2–8

FLOWERING Midsummer

L

Lilium formosanum var. *pricei* Formosa lily

THE SOLITARY, SCENTED FLOWERS—with luck there may be up to three—look like wide-open trumpets measuring up to 8in (20cm) long. They are white inside, and have a purple tinge outside. The parent, *Lilium formosanum*, needs a sunny, sheltered position or conservatory, but *L. formosanum* var. *pricei* is hardier and definitely the one for regions with cooler winters. If growing the taller *L. formosanum*, keep it in a pot and stand it outside over summer, putting it back in the conservatory over winter; grow as for 'African Queen' (*see page 160*).

PLANT PROFILE

HEIGHT 4–12in (10–30cm)

SITE Full sun

SOIL Fertile, free-draining

HARDINESS Z7–9 H8–4

FLOWERING Early midsummer

Lilium Golden Splendor Group Lily

L

THE STRONG, STURDY STEMS of *Lilium* Golden Splendor Group carry impressive clusters of large, outward-facing, scented flowers. They come in various shades of yellow, usually golden, with a dark burgundy stripe on the outside of each petal. An astonishing sight and quite tall, they can be used to full advantage in the middle to back ranks of a border, provided they do not obscure anything behind them. See 'African Queen' (*page 160*) for growing tips.

PLANT PROFILE	
HEIGHT 4–6ft (1.2–2m)	
SITE Full sun	
SOIL Fertile, free-draining	
HARDINESS Z3–8 H8–1	
FLOWERING Midsummer	

OTHER VARIETY *L.* 'Royal Gold' (richly scented, golden yellow).

L

Lilium hansonii Hanson's lily

A TOUGH AND BEAUTIFUL JAPANESE LILY with thick, almost fleshy, swept-back petals, in brilliant orange-yellow, bearing purple-brown spots. The nodding, early-summer flowers are nicely scented. *L. hansonii* needs to be grown in rich, free-draining soil in a part of the garden that excludes continuous, direct sun. In fact, growing it in light shade also brings out the best of the color, which tends to get washed out in the full glare of the sun. For growing tips, see 'African Queen' (*page 160*).

PLANT PROFILE

HEIGHT 3–5ft (1–1.5m)

SITE Partial shade

SOIL Fertile, free-draining

HARDINESS Z2–7 H7–1

FLOWERING Early summer

Lilium henryi Henry's lily

L

THE LARGE BULB OF THIS LILY produces strong stems with anywhere from 10 to 20 (if you are lucky) elegant, nodding, orange flowers up to 3in (8cm) wide. They have striking deep black spots and swept-back petals. A reliable, rough, tough plant, it is a good ingredient for late summer gardens, especially borders packed with brightly colored dahlias and brash yellow rudbeckias, and there should be no problems whatsoever in getting good results, provided you steer clear of acidic soil. See 'African Queen' (*page 160*) for growing tips.

OTHER VARIETY *L. speciosum* (pale pink or white flowers flushed deeper pink in the centers with pink or crimson spots).

PLANT PROFILE
HEIGHT 3–10ft (1–3m)
SITE Partial shade
SOIL Fertile, free-draining
HARDINESS Z3–8 H8–1
FLOWERING Late summer

L

Lilium 'Journey's End' Lily

IT'S A GOOD IDEA TO RESIST the temptation to buy nothing but midsummer-flowering lilies. 'Journey's End' produces large, deep pink flowers in late summer, with maroon spots and white at the margins and tips. Richly colored, it is just what you need when many other midseason border plants are past their best. 'Journey's End' also provides a lively link between the midsummer plants and those grown for their autumn colors. Grow as for 'African Queen' (*see page 160*).

OTHER VARIETY *L. davidii* (rich orange flowers with dark speckling).

PLANT PROFILE
HEIGHT 3–6ft (1–2m)
SITE Full sun
SOIL Fertile, free-draining
HARDINESS Z3–8 H8–1
FLOWERING Late summer

Lilium lancifolium Tiger lily

THE IMPRESSIVELY PROLIFIC *Lilium lancifolium* has three major advantages. First, it can produce up to 40 flowers (more likely 20, but you may be lucky) with orange-red petals and dark purple spots. Second, with a maximum height of 5ft (1.5m), it makes a superb show, visible across the garden. And third, the display of flowers opens at the end of summer and in early autumn when most other lilies are long finished. *L. lancifolium* var. *splendens* (*see inset*) is also impressive. Ideally, plant the bulbs in moist, acidic soil and see 'African Queen' (*page 160*) for growing tips.

OTHER VARIETY *L. lancifolium* var. *flaviflorum* (yellow flowers).

PLANT PROFILE	
HEIGHT 2–5ft (60–150cm)	
SITE Full sun	
SOIL Fertile, free-draining	
HARDINESS Z2–7 H7–1	
FLOWERING Late summer and early autumn	

L | *Lilium longiflorum* Easter lily

THE EASTER LILY IS VIRTUALLY ALWAYS SEEN as a florist's flower in extravagant wreaths and bouquets. It is strongly scented and exceptionally beautiful, with up to six funnel-like, pure white blooms. Unfortunately, *Lilium longiflorum* is far too tender for cool-climate gardens and needs to be grown in a pot. Keep it in a conservatory over winter, and only stand it outside after the last the frost, in late spring. For growing tips, see 'African Queen' (*page 160*).

OTHER VARIETY *L. regale* 'Album' (almost pure white flowers with some orange).

PLANT PROFILE

HEIGHT 16–39in (40–100cm)

SITE Partial shade

SOIL Fertile, free-draining

HARDINESS Z7–9 H9–1

FLOWERING Midsummer

Lilium mackliniae Lily

L

A LILY WITH A BIG DIFFERENCE, *L. mackliniae* has completely untypical rose pink flowers that resemble 2in- (6cm-) wide bells, each with a lovely purple–pink color outside, and white with rose pink within. The blooms appear in clusters of about six. All the experts love it, which is why it is always referred to as "choice" or "beautiful." Give it a prominent position toward the front of a cool, semishaded border, where it needs free-draining soil with plenty of added leaf mold. See 'African Queen' (*page 160*) for growing tips.

PLANT PROFILE

HEIGHT 12–24in (30–60cm)

SITE Full sun

SOIL Fertile, free-draining

HARDINESS Z7–8 H8–7

FLOWERING Early and midsummer

L

Lilium martagon Common turkscap lily

A QUIET, GENTLE, UNPRETENTIOUS LILY, *L. martagon* soon produces good clumps. It provides clusters of up to 50 small, pink to purple-red flowers with swept-back, speckled petals, although you are more likely to get half that number. *L. martagon* var. *album* (*see inset*) bears pure white flowers. Despite their unpleasant scent, the blooms make a free and easy show, dangling from the stiff, upright stem. For growing tips, see 'African Queen' (*page 160*). Free-draining soil is important, but the site can vary from dappled shade to full sun (in the wild, it grows in woodlands and open spaces).

PLANT PROFILE	
HEIGHT 3–6ft (1–2m)	
SITE Sun	
SOIL Fertile, free-draining	
HARDINESS Z3–8 H8–1	
FLOWERING Midsummer	

Lilium medeoloides Wheel lily

L

THE ORANGE-RED TO APRICOT, dark speckled flowers of *Lilium medeoloides* have attractive swept-back petals. Quite small for a lily, it reaches between knee- and thigh-height and is best placed at the front of a border where it can be clearly seen. This means you will have a good view of up to two whorls of leaves on the stem, with five to ten flowers appearing above them. See 'African Queen' (*page 160*) for growing tips. It needs acidic soil with partial shade, but if you don't have this in your garden, simply plant several in a container.

OTHER VARIETY *L. amabile* (red flowers with dark purple or black spots and some red-brown).

PLANT PROFILE

HEIGHT 16–30in (40–75cm)

SITE Partial shade

SOIL Fertile, free-draining, acidic

HARDINESS Z3–7 H7–1

FLOWERING Midsummer

Lilium monadelphum Caucasian lily

VERY IMPRESSIVE, WITH UP TO 30 large, trumpet-shaped flowers, measuring 4in (10cm) wide, yellow *Lilium monadelphum* is spotted maroon or purple inside, with a purple-brown flush outside. It scores over other lilies because it is one of the first to flower in early summer, when it gives off a lovely scent. It is quite happy in heavy ground and tolerates drier, sunnier conditions than most lilies. In short, you can't go wrong, especially on decent soil. Grow as for 'African Queen' (*see page 160*).

OTHER VARIETY *L. oxypetalum* (yellow flowers with purple dots).

PLANT PROFILE

HEIGHT 3–5ft (1–1.5)

SITE Full sun

SOIL Fertile, free-draining

HARDINESS Z5–8 H8–5

FLOWERING Early summer

Lilium nepalense Nepal lily

L

A SPECTACULARLY BEAUTIFUL LILY, which in temperate climates needs to be planted in greenhouse borders. *Lilium nepalense* cannot be grown in pots because it sends out horizontal underground stems, which then produce erect growth, with the early and midsummer flowers on top. They are stunning trumpet shapes, measuring about 6in (15cm) long and wide. The color is usually yellow, green-yellow, or green-white, with purple-burgundy markings. Make sure the soil has plenty of leaf mold. See 'African Queen' (*page 160*) for growing tips.

PLANT PROFILE	
HEIGHT 24–39in (60–100cm)	
SITE Partial shade	
SOIL Fertile, free-draining	
HARDINESS Z7–8 H8–7	
FLOWERING Early and midsummer	

L

Lilium pardalinum Leopard lily

IF YOU NEED A LILY to make bright, attractive clumps in a damp site with full sun or some shade, *Lilium pardalinum* is an excellent choice. It sends up strong, vertical stems with as many as ten nodding, flamboyant flowers that are orange-red to crimson with tightly swept-back petals. The petals are yellow-tangerine at the base with dark speckling, and have dark red markings at the tips. There are also dense whorls of leaves. Grow as for 'African Queen' (*see page 160*).

OTHER VARIETY *L. pardalinum* var. *giganteum* (crimson flowers, yellow toward the bases with crimson spots).

PLANT PROFILE
HEIGHT 5–8ft (1.5–2.5m)
SITE Full sun
SOIL Fertile, free-draining
HARDINESS Z5–8 H8–5
FLOWERING Midsummer

Lilium Pink Perfection Group Lily

L

THE ATTRACTIVE BLOOMS of *Lilium* Pink Perfection Group—and there might be 24–36 of them—are 6in (15cm) wide. They appear on top of impressive stems that measure up to 6ft (2m) high, making them ideal contenders for the middle or back ranks of a border. They also give a flash of flamboyant color to subtropical borders of large-leaved plants. In the 1960s, these bulbs were on the pink side, but the flowers are now much more likely to veer toward deep red or purple. For growing tips, see 'African Queen' (*page 160*).

OTHER VARIETY *L*. 'African Queen' (*see page160*).

PLANT PROFILE	
HEIGHT 5–6ft (1.5–2m)	
SITE Full sun	
SOIL Fertile, free-draining	
HARDINESS Z4–8 H8–1	
FLOWERING Midsummer	

L | *Lilium pumilum* Coral lily

IGNORE THE FACT that *Lilium pumilum* can be short-lived because
it is easy to buy replacement bulbs every few years, and they give
such a delightful show. The tiny bulbs send up grasslike leaves and
wiry stems (*see inset*) with up to 30 scented, almost glossy, small
scarlet flowers with swept-back petals. Growing only 6–18in
(15–45cm) high, *L. pumilum* needs to be planted toward the front of
a border or even in a rock garden, and requires acidic soil. For
growing tips, see 'African Queen' (*page 160*).

OTHER VARIETY *L. pumilum* 'Golden Gleam' (apricot-yellow flowers).

PLANT PROFILE

HEIGHT 6–18in (15–45cm)

SITE Full sun or
partial shade

SOIL Fertile, acidic,
free-draining

HARDINESS Z3–8 H8–1

FLOWERING Early summer

Lilium pyrenaicum Yellow turkscap lily

L

FORGET THE FACT that everyone says it reeks, because that is only a problem when you get your nose right into the flowers. From one step back, the big attraction of *Lilium pyrenaicum* is the sight of up to 12 dangling yellow or green-yellow flowers, with black-maroon lines and speckling. The obvious place for it is a border, but also try it in grass, which is how it grows in the wild in northern Spain. See 'African Queen' (*page 160*) for growing tips.

OTHER VARIETY L. 'Rosemary North' (ocher flowers with a few dark ocher spots on the outside).

PLANT PROFILE
HEIGHT 12–39in (30–100cm)
SITE Full sun
SOIL Fertile, free-draining
HARDINESS Z4–7 H7–1
FLOWERING Early and midsummer

L

Lilium regale Regal lily

THE REGAL IS ONE OF THE most striking and highly scented
lilies. It has up to 25 5–6in- (12–15cm-) long, trumpet-shaped
white flowers (flushed purple or purple-brown outside) with
yellow centers. Commonly regarded as the beginner's lily, because
it is so easy to grow and never lets you down, it produces first-rate
results. But if that suggests that only the most amateur of amateur
gardeners should grow it, think again. This is a superb lily that
reliably perks up borders in midsummer. For growing tips, see
'African Queen' (*page 160*).

OTHER VARIETY *L. longiflorum* (*see page 178*).

PLANT PROFILE	
HEIGHT 2–6ft (1–2m)	
SITE Full sun	
SOIL Fertile, free-draining	
HARDINESS Z3–8 H8–1	
FLOWERING Midsummer	

Lilium speciosum var. *album* Lily

L

A MUST FOR ANYONE wanting to prolong the lily season, *Lilium speciosum* var. *album* blooms in late summer and early autumn. It produces five to ten or more large, scented white flowers that are up to 7in (18cm) wide with swept-back petals. Extra color comes from the purple stems, while the leaves sometimes have margins with silver hairs. It also makes an excellent cut flower. Give it moist, acidic soil and a site out of full sun, and see 'African Queen' (*page 160*) for growing tips.

PLANT PROFILE

HEIGHT 3–5½ft (1–1.7m)

SITE Partial shade

SOIL Moist, acidic

HARDINESS Z3–8 H8–1

FLOWERING Late summer and early autumn

L

Lilium speciosum var. *rubrum* Red Japanese show lily

ADDING AN EXOTIC DASH to the late-summer and early-autumn garden, *Lilium speciosum* var. *rubrum* has five to ten or more large, scented, carmine red flowers, heavily speckled with red spots. They have swept-back petals and are up to 7in (18cm) wide, while the stems are purple-brown. It is very similar to *L. speciosum* var. *album* (*see page 189*); mix the two together for a striking red and white combination. Moist, acidic soil and a site out of full sun are essential; otherwise, grow as for 'African Queen' (*page 160*).

PLANT PROFILE

HEIGHT 3–5½ft (1–1.7m)

SITE Partial shade

SOIL Moist, acidic

HARDINESS Z3–8 H8–1

FLOWERING Late summer and early autumn

Lilium 'Star Gazer' Lily

L

RICHLY COLORED AND BEAUTIFULLY SCENTED, the red flowers of *Lilium* 'Star Gazer' are shaped like huge open stars. The petals have dark speckling, and there is a white mark around the edges. 'Star Gazer' also provides very good cut flowers. Try to plant the bulbs close to the edge of a bed where passersby can catch the scent. The best way to highlight the redness of the flowers is by growing white and pastel-colored lilies nearby. In bulb catalogs it is usually listed with the Oriental Hybrids, which include many excellent bulbs, such as the pure white 'Casa Blanca'. For growing tips, see 'African Queen' (*page 160*).

OTHER VARIETY *L.* 'Acapulco' (rose pink, lightly speckled with red).

PLANT PROFILE	
HEIGHT	3–5ft (1–1.5m)
SITE	Full sun
SOIL	Fertile, free-draining
HARDINESS	Z3–8 H8–1
FLOWERING	Midsummer

L

Lilium 'Sterling Star' Lily

EQUALLY GOOD USED FOR CUT FLOWERS or in a showy garden display, *Lilium* 'Sterling Star' has wide-open, star-shaped white blooms with attractive brown speckling toward the center. It makes a sharp combination with red- and blue-flowering plants and, if you get your nose in close, there is a very faint, sweet scent. A good choice for formal displays or free-and-easy cottage gardens. For growing tips, see 'African Queen' (*page 160*).

OTHER VARIETY *L.* 'Jetfire' (rich orange flowers and yellow centers).

PLANT PROFILE

HEIGHT 3–4ft (1–1.2m)

SITE Full sun

SOIL Fertile, free-draining

HARDINESS Z3–8 H8–1

FLOWERING Early and midsummer

Lilium superbum American turkscap lily

L

THIS EXTREMELY USEFUL LILY dates back to 1738 or even earlier. It flowers right at the start of autumn, and has the added advantage of hitting 10ft (3m) high with luck. There can be up to 40, but more likely 20, dangling flowers, with bright orange petals speckled with maroon spots, which appear like tropical butterflies fluttering above the foliage. *Lilium superbum* needs moist, acidic soil, and is ideal for the edge of a woodland. Grow as for 'African Queen' (*see page 160*).

PLANT PROFILE

HEIGHT 5–10ft (1.5–3m)

SITE Partial shade

SOIL Moist, acidic

HARDINESS Z4–8 H8–1

FLOWERING Late summer and early autumn

OTHER VARIETY *L. duchartrei* (*see page 169*).

M | *Merendera montana*

RARELY GETTING ABOVE ANKLE-HIGH, tiny *Merendera montana* needs to be grown in rock gardens, where it produces a star-shaped, purple to red-purple flower, with just a few 3in- (7cm-) long petals. Sometimes you might find an attractive white patch at the base of each. In fact, *M. montana* is so small that the base of the flower seems to sit right on the soil. In the wild, it grows in rocky or grassy sites in the Pyrenees; in the garden, it needs moist, free-draining soil.

PLANT PROFILE
HEIGHT 2in (5cm)
SPREAD 2in (5cm)
SITE Full sun
SOIL Moist but free-draining
HARDINESS Z6–9 H9–6
FLOWERING Autumn

Moraea huttonii Butterfly iris

M

EASY TO MISTAKE FOR A TRUE IRIS, the scented, South African *Moraea huttonii* has three outer and three inner petals colored golden yellow with brown marks toward the center. Because it flowers in the spring, it might be caught by frosts, so it needs to be grown in a conservatory unless you have a very mild, sheltered garden. Plant the bulbs 3in (7cm) deep in spring or autumn in rich, free-draining soil where there is some shade from the midday sun. Water sparingly as growth begins, then freely when in full growth. Dry off as the leaves wither to ensure that it is dry during dormancy, from midsummer to autumn.

OTHER VARIETY *M. spathulata* (golden yellow flowers).

PLANT PROFILE

HEIGHT 28–36in (70–90cm)

SPREAD 3in (8cm)

SITE Full sun, midday shade

SOIL Rich in organic matter, free-draining

HARDINESS Z9–10 H10–9

FLOWERING Spring to early summer

M | *Moraea polystachya* Butterfly iris

A TENDER SOUTH AFRICAN PLANT, *Moraea polystachya* has violet to pale blue flowers, just like those of an iris. The three outer petals have a yellow mark in the center with a white margin. To grow outside, it needs a mild garden where temperatures do not slip below freezing. It also needs free-draining soil and a position at the foot of a sunny wall where the ground does not get too wet over winter. Otherwise, plant *M. polystachya* in a pot with a loam-based potting mix and added sharp sand. Water sparingly as the growth begins, then freely in full growth. Reduce watering as the leaves wither, and keep dry when dormant.

OTHER VARIETY *M. natalensis* (lilac or violet-blue flowers with yellow central marks ringed with mauve).

PLANT PROFILE	
HEIGHT 32in (80cm)	
SPREAD 3in (8cm)	
SITE Full sun	
SOIL Average, rich in organic matter, free-draining	
HARDINESS Z9–10	
FLOWERING Summer	

Muscari armeniacum Grape hyacinth

M

REMARKABLY EASY TO GROW, *Muscari armeniacum* produces attractive short spikes packed with tiny, white-mouthed, bright blue flowers (*see inset*) above its grasslike leaves. It flowers in spring, so try using it to liven up the ground around deciduous shrubs before they start performing in late spring and early summer. For best results, plant them in autumn, 4in (10cm) deep in slightly moist but free-draining soil. The bulbs soon produce congested clumps that need tackling. During their summer dormancy, gently pry them out of the ground and divide the clump, replanting the outer bulbs; if you don't, the flowers will eventually be obscured by the leaves.

OTHER VARIETY *M. armeniacum* 'Argaei Album' (white; flowers later).

PLANT PROFILE
HEIGHT 8in (20cm)
SPREAD 2in (5cm)
SITE Full sun
SOIL Fertile, moist but free-draining
HARDINESS Z6–9 H9–5
FLOWERING Spring

M | *Muscari armeniacum* 'Blue Spike' Grape hyacinth

ALTHOUGH IT LOOKS JUST LIKE ITS PARENT, *Muscari armeniacum* (*see page 197*), and enjoys similar growing conditions, the large, blue flowers of 'Blue Spike' are double and more tightly packed together. Being small, it is invariably grown toward the front of a garden or used around deciduous shrubs before they come into their own and start grabbing the eye in late spring and early summer, at which point the grape hyacinth will be entering its dormant phase and taking a rest.

OTHER VARIETY *M. armeniacum* 'Fantasy Creation' (sky blue flowers that take on a faint green tinge).

PLANT PROFILE
HEIGHT 8in (20cm)
SPREAD 2in (5cm)
SITE Full sun
SOIL Average, moist but free-draining
HARDINESS Z4–8 H8–1
FLOWERING Spring

Muscari aucheri Grape hyacinth

M

EQUALLY INTERESTING TO BOTANISTS and amateur gardeners, this Turkish plant can be seen to have two kinds of tiny flowers in a single cluster, if you peer in and take a close look. At the top of the spike are infertile pale blue flowers, while below are bright blue ones with white mouths. You probably won't be able to make this distinction from a distance; all you will see is small flowers just above the thin leaves, making a gentle patch of color at the front of the border.

PLANT PROFILE

HEIGHT 4–6in (10–15cm)

SPREAD 2in (5cm)

SITE Full sun

SOIL Average, moist but free-draining

HARDINESS Z6–9 H9–5

FLOWERING Spring

M | *Muscari botryoides* 'Album' Grape hyacinth

THIS SCENTED, WHITE GRAPE HYACINTH mixes well with its blue parent *Muscari botryoides*, and makes a lively contrast. The effect is enhanced by the relatively small number of distracting, spoon-shaped leaves, sometimes just three per bulb. It likes cool sites, with moist, free-draining soil. Its low height necessitates a position right at the front of a garden, and it is often used in a narrow borders with a path on one side and a lawn on the other.

OTHER VARIETY *M. armeniacum* 'Saffier' (dark blue with a white edge).

PLANT PROFILE
HEIGHT 6–8in (15–20cm)
SPREAD 2in (5cm)
SITE Full sun
SOIL Average, moist but free-draining
HARDINESS Z2–8 H8–1
FLOWERING Spring

Muscari macrocarpum Grape hyacinth

M

AN INTRIGUING KIND OF GRAPE HYACINTH, *Muscari macrocarpum* has banana-scented flowers that look like tiny tubes pointing outward. The buds are purple-brown, but when the flowers open, they are yellow. It is originally from the Aegean islands and is not totally hardy, but given a sunny, sheltered, frost-free site at the base of a wall where it can bake over summer and very free-draining ground, it should survive without any problems in cooler regions.

PLANT PROFILE

HEIGHT 4–6in (10–15cm)	
SPREAD 3in (8cm)	
SITE Full sun	
SOIL Average, moist but free-draining	
HARDINESS Z7–9 H9–7	
FLOWERING Spring	

N | *Narcissus* 'Acropolis' Daffodil

THIS INTERESTING DAFFODIL has snowy white petals and a few orange-red ones in the middle. When planting daffodils in grass, roll back the turf in autumn and plant the bulbs one-and-a-half to two times their own depth, in a sunny position, 8–12in (20–30cm) apart. They need at least 6in (15cm) of soil above because in mid- and late spring, in periods without any rain, the topsoil quickly dries. Below that level, the bulbs can fatten and drink all they want. Well-drained ground is essential, and fine grass is better than choking, vigorous growth. On poor soils, sprinkle all-purpose fertilizer after flowering, but before the foliage dies, and snip off the flowers as they fade.

OTHER VARIETY *N.* 'Gay Kybo' (creamy white with rich orange).

PLANT PROFILE
HEIGHT 18in (45cm)
SPREAD 6in (15cm)
SITE Full sun or dappled, part-day shade
SOIL Average, moist but free-draining
HARDINESS Z3–9 H9–1
FLOWERING Midspring

Narcissus 'Actaea' Daffodil

A PARTICULARLY ATTRACTIVE, striking daffodil, which has a flat, open, bright white flower with six petals, and a tiny yellow eye in the middle with neat red edging. Plant *Narcissus* 'Actaea' in bold groups at the foot of ornamental trees with attractive dark bark, such as the shiny brown *Prunus serrula*, at the base of dark brown wooden structures, or in wooden tubs, making an excellent contrast for late spring. For growing tips, see 'Acropolis' (*opposite*).

OTHER VARIETY *N.* 'Cantabile' (white flowers with red-rimmed, green and yellow cups).

PLANT PROFILE
HEIGHT 18in (45cm)
SPREAD 6in (15cm)
SITE Full sun or dappled, part-day shade
SOIL Average, moist but free-draining
HARDINESS Z3–9 H9–1
FLOWERING Late spring

N | *Narcissus* 'Binkie' Daffodil

THE FLOWERS OPEN with clear, lemon-colored petals in the middle of spring, after which the central cups gradually fade to creamy white. *Narcissus* 'Binkie' is a very good choice for growing in bold sweeps in grass, where it multiplies well, for encircling and highlighting statues and other stylish, ornamental effects, and for flanking the sides of a path and the approach to a house. It is a strong, robust plant, ideal for cottage and formal gardens where it will not get beaten down by heavy downpours. For growing tips, see 'Acropolis' (*page 202*).

OTHER VARIETY *N.* 'Carlton' (soft yellow with a frilled trumpet).

PLANT PROFILE
HEIGHT 14in (35cm)
SPREAD 6in (15cm)
SITE Full sun or dappled, part-day shade
SOIL Average, moist but free-draining
HARDINESS Z3–9 H9–1
FLOWERING Midspring

Narcissus 'Broadway Star' Daffodil

THIS DAFFODIL IS AN INCREASINGLY popular choice due to its background of white petals and the unusual, highly distinctive array of orange stripes right in the center (some catalogs call them bright red). A robust grower, 'Broadway Star' is worth planting in large groups on an open lawn, though it can be used with equal success to highlight any garden feature. Traditionalists may prefer a good dose of yellow, but for a novel touch, 'Broadway Star' comes highly recommended. See 'Acropolis' (*page 202*) for growing tips.

OTHER VARIETY *N.* 'Orangery' (creamy white flowers with an orange center).

PLANT PROFILE

HEIGHT 16in (40cm)

SPREAD 6in (15cm)

SITE Full sun or dappled part-day shade

SOIL Average, moist but free-draining

HARDINESS Z3–9 H9–1

FLOWERING Midspring

N | *Narcissus bulbocodium* Hoop-petticoat daffodil

A GEM OF A SMALL DAFFODIL, *Narcissus bulbocodium* has tiny, funnel-shaped, deep yellow flowers that last a long time in midspring. Since it is so small, it needs a prominent position; rock gardens are ideal because it needs to be kept on the dry side in summer. It can also be grown in pots, or in front of Mediterranean shrubs and others with similar requirements, like Mexican orange blossom (*Choisya ternata*), that do not need lavish watering in a dry summer. Allow *N. bulbocodium* to spread by leaving the flowers to scatter seed. For growing tips, see 'Acropolis' (*page 202*).

OTHER VARIETY *N. bulbocodium* var. *citrinus* (pale lemon yellow).

PLANT PROFILE

HEIGHT 4–6in (10–15cm)

SPREAD To 2in (5cm)

SITE Full sun or dappled, part-day shade

SOIL Average, moist but free-draining, slightly acidic

HARDINESS Z3–9 H9–1

FLOWERING Midspring

Narcissus cantabricus White hoop-petticoat daffodil

N

ONE OF THE EARLIEST-FLOWERING and shortest daffodils, *Narcissus cantabricus* is a million miles away from the bright, brash, golden yellow daffodils found in public parks. The funnel-shaped white flowers are just 1½in (3.5cm) wide, and the 6in- (15cm-) long leaves are grass- or chivelike. It is best grown in rock gardens where it can be clearly seen. Failing that, make sure it has a prominent position toward the front of a border. See 'Acropolis' (*page 202*) for growing tips.

OTHER VARIETY *N. cantabricus* subsp. *cantabricus* var. *foliosus* (milk white flowers with a wavy-edged cup).

PLANT PROFILE
HEIGHT 6–8in (15–20cm)
SITE Full sun or dappled, part-day shade
SOIL Average, moist but free-draining
HARDINESS Z3–9 H9–1
FLOWERING Winter

N *Narcissus* 'Chanterelle' Daffodil

THIS IS A GOOD CHOICE for its large, eye-catching flowers, which have white petals with a patch of bright yellow. *Narcissus* 'Chanterelle' makes a flashy change from the traditional egg-yolk yellow daffodils that are suddenly everywhere in spring. It can easily be grown in clumps to create an effective contrast with two other kinds, those in bright yellow and others in shades of orange. For growing tips see 'Acropolis' (*page 202*).

OTHER VARIETY *N.* 'Cassata' (flowers in midspring).

PLANT PROFILE
HEIGHT 16in (40cm)
SPREAD 6in (15cm)
SITE Full sun or dappled, part-day shade
SOIL Average, moist but free-draining, slightly acidic
HARDINESS Z4–8
FLOWERING Mid-spring

Narcissus 'Cheerfulness' Daffodil

N

THE LOVELY, SWEET SCENT of *Narcissus* 'Cheerfulness' means it needs to be grown in a sheltered, sunny position where the scent can hang in the air and will not get blown away. The flowers appear in small clusters, and are creamy white with a pale yellow eye; 'Yellow Cheerfulness' (*see inset*) is entirely yellow. Both varieties are suitable for growing in windowboxes and containers; position pots on tables in patios or courtyards to enjoy the scent without bending down. If possible, provide a dark background so that the flowers stand out. See 'Acropolis' (*page 202*) for growing tips.

OTHER VARIETY *N.* 'Petit Four' (milk white flowers with an apricot-rose cup).

PLANT PROFILE	
HEIGHT 16in (40cm)	
SPREAD 6in (15cm)	
SITE Full sun or dappled, part-day shade	
SOIL Average, moist but free-draining	
HARDINESS Z3–9 H9–1	
FLOWERING Midspring	

Narcissus cyclamineus Daffodil

THE TINY, DANGLING FLOWERS of *Narcissus cyclamineus* have tightly swept-back petals and a thin, protruding trumpet, up to ⅘in (2cm) long. Let *N. cyclamineus* grow and multiply in moist parts of the garden—for example, fairly close to natural ponds, where the grass is on the lush side but not so vigorous that the short flowers are in any way swamped or hidden. The best way to encourage this robust daffodil to spread and make attractive clumps is to delay cutting off the dead flowers until the seed has scattered. Grow as for 'Acropolis' (*see page 202*).

OTHER VARIETY *N. triandrus* (cream flowers).

PLANT PROFILE

HEIGHT 6–8in (15–20cm)

SPREAD To 3in (8cm)

SITE Full sun or dappled, part-day shade

SOIL Average, moist but free-draining, slightly acidic

HARDINESS Z3–9 H9–1

FLOWERING Early spring

Narcissus 'Daydream' Daffodil

N

THE ATTRACTIVE FLOWERS of *Narcissus* 'Daydream' have a mix of green-yellow petals, and a central cup with a ring of white at the base. By the end of spring the cups have turned white. To make the flowers really stand out, it helps if they are placed with an evergreen hedge or shrub in the background. Alternatively, grow clusters of 'Daydream' among an array of tulips with strong colors, such as rich red and deep mauve or purple. See 'Acropolis' (*page 202*) for growing tips.

PLANT PROFILE
HEIGHT 14in (35cm)
SPREAD 6in (15cm)
SITE Full sun or dappled, part-day shade
SOIL Average, moist but free-draining
HARDINESS Z3–7
FLOWERING Midspring

N *Narcissus* 'Dove Wings' Daffodil

THE FLOWERS OF *Narcissus* 'Dove Wings' are a combination of creamy white, swept-back petals and lemon yellow protruding cups. The overall effect is thoroughly modest and restrained, and it can be used to tone things down when other parts of the garden have much more brashly colored, early spring tulips. 'Dove Wings' can also be grown to make an instant foreground contrast with dark evergreen shrubs behind, and to fringe a path leading into a stylish, elegant part of the garden. For growing tips, see 'Acropolis' (*page 202*).

OTHER VARIETY *N.* 'Charity May' (lemon yellow flowers).

PLANT PROFILE

HEIGHT 12in (30cm)

SPREAD 3in (8cm)

SITE Full sun or dappled, part-day shade

SOIL Average, moist but free-draining

HARDINESS Z3–9 H9–1

FLOWERING Early spring

Narcissus 'February Gold' Daffodil

N

A HIGHLY SUCCESSFUL OLD VARIETY that is still going strong, *Narcissus* 'February Gold' has yellow petals and a slightly deeper, stronger yellow cup. It is one of the first daffodils to flower in early spring, though 'March Gold' would be a more appropriate name. At 12in (30cm) high, it is not one of the larger, more dominating daffodils, but it still makes an extremely attractive show, and it can also be grown in windowboxes. 'February Silver' (*see inset*) is also worth a try. Grow as for 'Acropolis' (*see page 202*).

OTHER VARIETY *N.* 'Jenny' (creamy white flowers with lemon yellow trumpets).

PLANT PROFILE		
HEIGHT 12in (30cm)		
SPREAD 3in (8cm)		
SITE Full sun or dappled, part-day shade		
SOIL Average, moist but free-draining		
HARDINESS Z3–9 H9–1		
FLOWERING Early spring		

N *Narcissus* 'Golden Ducat' Daffodil

THE BROAD, DEEP YELLOW PETALS of *Narcissus* 'Gold Ducat' resemble the shape of a star and are its key attraction. They combine well with sweetly scented pink or blue hyacinths or with richly colored tulips, the bulk of which come into flower in midspring, to create a multicolored show. A valuable alternative to the traditional kind of daffodil, with its highly distinctive central trumpet, 'Golden Ducat' is certainly worth growing in cottage or informal gardens and using in cut-flower displays. For growing tips, see 'Acropolis' (*page 202*).

PLANT PROFILE

HEIGHT 14in (35cm)

SPREAD 4in (10cm)

SITE Full sun or dappled, part-day shade

SOIL Average, moist but free-draining

HARDINESS Z3–9 H9–1

FLOWERING Midspring

Narcissus 'Golden Harvest' Daffodil

N

AN EXCELLENT, LARGE, ROBUST FLOWER that is bright golden yellow and opens from early spring to midspring, although it can be forced for midwinter blooms. *Narcissus* 'Golden Harvest' always puts on a good display, and is excellent for growing in grass, where it quickly multiplies. It is worth ensuring that the clumps can be seen from windows overlooking the garden so that you catch a glimpse of 'Golden Harvest' whether you are inside or out. Plant groups of bulbs wherever the spring garden needs a lift. See 'Acropolis' (*page 202*) for growing tips.

OTHER VARIETY *N.* 'Arkle' (largest of the yellow trumpet daffodils).

PLANT PROFILE	
HEIGHT 18in (45cm)	
SPREAD 4in (10cm)	
SITE Full sun or dappled, part-day shade	
SOIL Average, moist but free-draining	
HARDINESS Z3–7	
FLOWERING Early to midspring	

N | *Narcissus* 'Grand Soleil d' Or' Daffodil

THE TWO MAIN ATTRACTIONS of *Narcissus* 'Grand Soleil d'Or' are its sweet scent and the many gold and tangerine orange flowers that appear on each stem. The only potential problem is that it flowers in early spring, and can get caught by frosts, so make sure you plant it in a sheltered, sunny area where it is well protected from cold snaps, and where the scent can hang in the air. 'Grand Soleil d'Or' also makes good cut flowers. In bulb catalogs, it is usually listed with the Poetaz group of daffodils. The bulbs need to bake over summer, but otherwise grow as for 'Acropolis' (*see page 202*).

OTHER VARIETY *N.* 'Geranium' (white petals with orange-red cups).

PLANT PROFILE
HEIGHT 18in (45cm)
SPREAD 3in (8cm)
SITE Sun
SOIL Average, moist but free-draining
HARDINESS Z7–9 H9–7
FLOWERING Early spring

Narcissus 'Hawera' Daffodil

A BEAUTIFUL DAFFODIL with a slender habit (*see inset*), *Narcissus* 'Hawera' features several stems per bulb, each one carrying up to five attractive, canary yellow flowers. They start opening in midspring and provide a small-scale, dainty show that needs to be placed right at the front of a border, in a rock garden, or in a windowbox so that it can be fully seen. 'Hawera' can also be grown in gaps in patio paving or a flagstone path and in pots that you can move to more prominent positions as the flowers open. See 'Acropolis' (*page 202*) for the best growing conditions.

OTHER VARIETY *N.* 'Tuesday's Child' (pointed white petals with lemon yellow cups).

PLANT PROFILE	
HEIGHT 7in (18cm)	
SPREAD 3in (8cm)	
SITE Sun	
SOIL Average, moist but free-draining	
HARDINESS Z3–9 H9–1	
FLOWERING Late spring	

Narcissus 'Ice Wings' Daffodil

THE NAME IS ENTIRELY ACCURATE because *Narcissus* 'Ice Wings' has neat white flowers, each with a pronounced central cup. Give the bulbs a dark green background, such as topiarized shrubs or an evergreen hedge, so that the colors can be seen to best effect, or try it in clusters with other clumps of bright yellow and orange daffodils. The relatively small flowers are just 1½in (4cm) wide, making 'Ice Wings' a good choice if you're after a small-scale effect—for example, around a miniature statue—or have a small garden. Grow as for 'Acropolis' (*see page 202*).

OTHER VARIETY *N.* 'Thalia' (milk white flowers).

PLANT PROFILE
HEIGHT 14in (35cm)
SITE Sun
SOIL Average, moist but free-draining
HARDINESS Z3–9 H9–1
FLOWERING Midspring

Narcissus 'Jack Snipe' Daffodil

N

MAY BE SHORT, but the flowers of *Narcissus* 'Jack Snipe' are long-
sting with white petals and lemon yellow trumpets. If it is being
own where it can spread (which it quickly does), plant the bulbs
ward the front of a border, in short and not-too-vigorous grass,
rock gardens and on banks and slopes, although it is also suitable
r pots and window boxes. It looks good planted in the foreground
ith more richly colored tulips behind. For growing tips, see
cropolis' (*page 202*).

THER VARIETY *N.* 'February Silver' (white petals with large, lemon
llow trumpets).

PLANT PROFILE	
HEIGHT 8in (20cm)	
SPREAD 3in (8cm)	
SITE Sun	
SOIL Average, moist but free-draining	
HARDINESS Z3–9 H9–1	
FLOWERING Early and midspring	

N | *Narcissus* 'Jetfire' Daffodil

WITH ITS EXCELLENT COMBINATION of golden yellow, swept-back petals, and long, bright orange trumpets, the only drawback of *Narcissus* 'Jetfire' is that its color tends to fade in bright sun. Only 8in (20cm) high, it is a very a good choice for small-scale gardening in tubs and rock gardens, and has quite a showy presence. It also makes a bright contrast against any blue garden structure, like the painted legs of a wooden pergola, or mixed with any of the early-flowering bright blue scillas, such as hardy *S. siberica*, which are about the same height. Grow as for 'Acropolis' (*see page 202*).

OTHER VARIETY *N.* 'Little Witch' (*see page 223*).

PLANT PROFILE
HEIGHT 8in (20cm)
SITE Sun
SOIL Average, moist but free-draining
HARDINESS Z3–9 H9–1
FLOWERING Early sprin

Narcissus jonquilla Wild jonquil

WILD JONQUIL NEEDS A SHELTERED hot spot in the garden so that it can thrive and you can enjoy its strong, sweet scent. The golden yellow flowers are small and unobtrusive at 1¼in (3cm) wide. Grown indoors in pots and given special care, it will flower early, but this is a very meticulous process. Given that they are so inexpensive, let the experts do the hard work behind the scenes and buy them in bud from garden centers. See 'Acropolis' (*page 202*) for growing tips. It can also be potted up in late summer; when the roots are growing well, put it on a windowsill for Christmas flowering.

OTHER VARIETY *N.* 'Baby Moon' (each stem carries several scented yellow flowers).

PLANT PROFILE
HEIGHT 12in (30cm)
SITE Full sun
SOIL Average, moist but fast-draining
HARDINESS Z3–9 H9–1
FLOWERING Late spring

N *Narcissus* 'Jumblie' Daffodil

EACH BULB OF *Narcissus* 'Jumblie' produces several stems carrying up to three nodding flowers. The pert, bright yellow petals are swept back, exposing the yellow-orange cups. Note that it is both small and not entirely hardy, which means that it needs a prominent position where it will not get hit by frost. Plant the bulbs toward the front of a border, to edge paths, and in gaps in patio paving, as well as in rock gardens, windowboxes, and pots. 'Jumblie' is a nice addition to small-scale, intricate parts of the garden, though it can also be used to set off groups of larger spring bulbs. For growing tips, see 'Acropolis' (*page 202*).

OTHER VARIETY *N.* 'Quince' (*see page 230*).

PLANT PROFILE
HEIGHT 7in (17cm)
SPREAD 2–3in (5–8cm)
SITE Sun
SOIL Average, moist but free-draining
HARDINESS Z3–9 H9–1
FLOWERING Early spring

Narcissus 'Little Witch' Daffodil

EQUALLY IMPRESSIVE GROWING IN SHORT, not-too-vigorous grass and around shrubs in the border, the golden yellow *Narcissus* 'Little Witch' gives a long-lasting show of flowers. The central cup seems to poke forward out of the swept-back petals. On the short side, it can be grown in various containers, from tubs to windowboxes, as well as in small-scale plantings—for example, in a courtyard. See 'Acropolis' (*page 202*) for growing tips.

OTHER VARIETY *N.* 'Peeping Tom' (golden yellow flowers).

PLANT PROFILE
HEIGHT 9in (22cm)
SITE Sun
SOIL Average, moist but free-draining
HARDINESS Z3–9 H9–1
FLOWERING Early and midspring

N | *Narcissus* 'Merlin' **Daffodil**

STRIKINGLY BEAUTIFUL, *Narcissus* 'Merlin' has flat, pure white petals arranged around a bright yellow cup edged with bright red. A nice, tall daffodil, it immediately catches the eye. Plant it in bold groups in parts of the garden where nothing else is really happening to create an instant feature and jazz things up, and to embellish other parts of the garden with a lively look. 'Merlin' makes a strong contrast to the deeper yellow- and orange-colored daffodils. For growing tips, see 'Acropolis' (*page 202*).

OTHER VARIETY *N.* 'Audubon' (white petals with a pink-edged, lemon yellow cup).

PLANT PROFILE
HEIGHT 18in (45cm)
SITE Sun
SOIL Average, moist but free-draining
HARDINESS Z3–9 H9–1
FLOWERING Midspring

Narcissus 'Minnow' Daffodil

N

A TOUGH, SMALL, HIGHLY RATED DAFFODIL, *Narcissus* 'Minnow' has cream-colored petals and pale yellow cups that gradually fade to cream. The only problem is that while it spreads well, some bulbs might not flower, which means you won't get any scent. The best position is a sunny border or rock garden backed by a sheltering wall, especially in a mild region where it can bake over summer. See 'Acropolis' (*page 202*) for growing tips. It can also be potted in late summer; when the roots are growing well, put it on a bright windowsill for Christmas flowering.

OTHER VARIETY *N.* 'Bridal Crown' (white flowers with orange-yellow in the centers).

PLANT PROFILE		
HEIGHT 7in (18cm)		
SITE Full sun		
SOIL Average, moist but free-draining		
HARDINESS Z3–9 H9–1		
FLOWERING Midspring		

N *Narcissus* 'Mount Hood' Daffodil

GIVING A STRONG SHOW, *Narcissus* 'Mount Hood' has white petals and a slightly flared, creamy white trumpet that gradually fades to off-white. It makes a bright contrast to red and mauve-purple tulips, against neat shrubs with glossy evergreen leaves, and those with bright red foliage in the spring, such as *Photinia x fraseri* 'Red Robin'. Keep it well away from a white background or you will never see it, but do plant it in front of any strongly colored wall or fence. For growing tips, see 'Acropolis' (*page 202*).

OTHER VARIETY *N.* 'Empress of Ireland' (large white flowers).

PLANT PROFILE

HEIGHT 18in (45cm)

SPREAD 6in (15cm)

SITE Sun

SOIL Average, moist but free-draining

HARDINESS Z3–9 H9–1

FLOWERING Midspring

Narcissus 'Pipit' Daffodil

THE ADVANTAGE OF GROWING THE 10in- (25cm-) high *Narcissus* 'Pipit' is that it flowers in the middle and second half of spring when there is more chance of warm, still days. And that is exactly what you need to appreciate its sweet scent. Plant the bulbs on the sunny side of a courtyard garden, at the foot of a south-facing wall, or in clusters along the foot of an evergreen hedge, which provides an excellent background color to the lemon yellow flowers that quickly fade to cream. See 'Acropolis' (*page 202*) for growing tips.

OTHER VARIETY *N.* 'Sun Disc' (rounded, rich yellow flowers).

PLANT PROFILE

HEIGHT 10in (25cm)

SPREAD 3in (8cm)

SITE Sun

SOIL Average, moist but free-draining

HARDINESS Z3–9 H9–1

FLOWERING Mid- and late spring

N | *Narcissus poeticus* var. *recurvus* **Old pheasant's eye**

ONE OF THE MOST BEAUTIFUL and popular daffodils, old pheasant's eye has swept-back, pure white, scented petals, a tiny green eye, and a central yellow cup edged with orange-red, and looks similar to its close relative *N. poeticus* 'Praecox' (*see inset*). Old pheasant's eye prefers slightly damper ground than most daffodils (especially in spring, otherwise it may not flower), and needs deep planting in rich soil where it will make a superb colony. If it is planted too close to the soil surface, the ground may be too dry if there is not much rain. For growing tips, see 'Acropolis' (*page 202*).

OTHER VARIETY *N. poeticus* 'Plenus' (fragrant, pure white flowers).

PLANT PROFILE

HEIGHT 14in (35cm)

SPREAD 4in (10cm)

SITE Full sun

SOIL Average, moist but free-draining

HARDINESS Z3–9 H9–1

FLOWERING Late spring

Narcissus 'Professor Einstein' **Daffodil**

ONE OF THE MOST STRIKING DAFFODILS, *Narcissus* 'Professor Einstein' has bright white, long-lasting flowers and a contrasting, large orange-red cup in the middle. As with most white daffodils, it benefits enormously from being planted in front of a glossy evergreen hedge or a group of shrubs, so that the color really stands out. See 'Acropolis' (*page 202*) for growing tips. 'Professor Einstein' can also be potted in late summer; when the roots are growing well, put it on a bright windowsill for a display of Christmas flowers.

OTHER VARIETY N. 'Kilworth' (white with red-orange centers).

PLANT PROFILE
HEIGHT 16in (40cm)
SPREAD 6in (16cm)
SITE Sun
SOIL Average, moist but free-draining
HARDINESS Z3–9 H9–1
FLOWERING midspring

N | *Narcissus* 'Quince' **Daffodil**

TO GET A GOOD SHOW OF THE richly colored, golden yellow flowers, make sure *Narcissus* 'Quince' is planted in a sunny, sheltered site in a mild garden. There are two or three flowers per stem. They make an effective contrast when planted around a tree trunk with shiny brown or greenish bark, such as the rich maroon-brown *Prunus serrula* or the green and white striped *Acer davidii*. For growing tips, see 'Acropolis' (*page 202*). 'Quince' can also be potted up in late summer; when the roots are growing well, put it on a windowsill for Christmas flowering.

OTHER VARIETY *N*. 'Jumblie' (*see page 222*).

PLANT PROFILE
HEIGHT 6in (16cm)
SPREAD 4in (10cm)
SITE Sun
SOIL Average, moist but free-draining
HARDINESS Z3–9 H9–1
FLOWERING Early and midspring

Narcissus 'Rip van Winkle' Daffodil

BIZARRE, QUIRKY, AND POPULAR, with its thin, spindly, star-shaped, green-yellow petals, *Narcissus* 'Rip van Winkle' looks more like a mini cactus dahlia than a daffodil. Highlight its shape by growing small groups where they can be clearly seen, ideally against a background in a contrasting color. Since 'Rip van Winkle' barely grows above ankle-height, it is a good choice for gaps in patio paving, rock gardens, windowboxes, and narrow borders flanking a path. See 'Acropolis' (*page 202*) for growing tips.

PLANT PROFILE	
HEIGHT 5½in (14cm)	
SPREAD 3in (8cm)	
SITE Sun	
SOIL Average, moist but free-draining	
HARDINESS Z3–9 H9–1	
FLOWERING Spring	

N | *Narcissus romieuxii* Daffodil

THIS PALE, FUNNEL-SHAPED DAFFODIL, from straw to primrose yellow, comes from North Africa and needs a sheltered, sunny hot spot if it is to thrive. Grow it in rock gardens to guarantee fast drainage (in gardens with heavy clay soil, it is best grown in pots or rock gardens with specially added light soil), and where it can easily be seen, because it will not get any higher than 4in (10cm). The narrow dark green leaves make a nice contrast with the yellow petals. *Narcissus romieuxii* is well worth growing for its early spring display. For growing tips, see 'Acropolis' (*page 202*).

OTHER VARIETY *N. romieuxii* 'Atlas Gold' (golden yellow flowers).

PLANT PROFILE

HEIGHT To 4in (10cm)

SPREAD 2in (5cm)

SITE Sun

SOIL Average, moist but free-draining

HARDINESS Z3–9 H9–1

FLOWERING Early spring

Narcissus rupicola Rock daffodil

N

AN EXQUISITE LITTLE WILD DAFFODIL from Portugal and Spain, *Narcissus rupicola* has a golden yellow face with six petals, a small central cup, and gray-green leaves. It is found on stony, rocky ground in the Mediterranean, so it needs a free-draining garden site, and is best grown at the front of sunny raised beds, which eliminate the need to bend down to catch the gentle scent, in rockeries or pots of a loam-based potting mix with plenty of added sand. Whatever happens, do not let the bulbs sit in sopping wet mud all winter. Grow as for 'Acropolis' (*see page 202*).

OTHER VARIETY *N. rupicola* subsp. *marvieri* (a very similar North African daffodil with green leaves).

PLANT PROFILE	
HEIGHT 6in (15cm)	
SPREAD 2–3in (5–8cm)	
SITE Sun	
SOIL Average, moist but free-draining	
HARDINESS Z3–9 H9–1	
FLOWERING Midspring	

N | *Narcissus* 'Silver Chimes' Daffodil

THERE ARE FROM SIX TO TEN nodding, scented, creamy white flowers on each sturdy stem of *Narcissus* 'Silver Chimes'. The central cup is a quiet, pale primrose yellow. In mild regions, provide a sunny border backed by a sheltering wall where it can bake over summer. 'Silver Chimes' also makes good cut flowers. In specialist bulb catalogs, it is listed with the Tazetta daffodils, which have small, usually scented flowers. For growing tips, see 'Acropolis' (*page 202*). It can also be potted in late summer; when the roots are growing well, put it on a windowsill for a Christmas show.

OTHER VARIETY *N.* 'Avalanche' (pure white petals with lemon yellow cups).

PLANT PROFILE

HEIGHT 12in (30cm)

SPREAD 3in (8cm)

SITE Full sun

SOIL Average, moist but free-draining

HARDINESS Z3–9 H9–1

FLOWERING Mid- and late spring

Narcissus 'Spellbinder' Daffodil

A THOROUGHLY TRADITIONAL DAFFODIL with an array of petals and a bold, trumpetlike cup in the middle. For lovers of yellow, *Narcissus* 'Spellbinder' is brilliantly brash, although it does fade slightly. Very vigorous, it makes an eye-catching clump in open lawns, in borders, or among fruit trees. There are many excellent alternatives, including *N.* 'Kingscourt' and *N.* 'Rijnveld's Early Sensation', which flower in midwinter when the weather is mild, or during late winter when it is colder. See 'Acropolis' (*page 202*) for growing tips.

PLANT PROFILE

HEIGHT 20in (50cm)

SPREAD 4in (10cm)

SITE Sun

SOIL Average, moist but free-draining

HARDINESS Z3–9 H9–1

FLOWERING Midspring

N | *Narcissus* 'Saint Keverne' Daffodil

AN EXTREMELY RELIABLE, large-cupped, golden yellow daffodil, *Narcissus* 'Saint Keverne' gives a good show year after year. It makes a lively clump in the open lawn, and in any area where the spring garden needs jazzing up with patches of flashy yellow. Try planting bold groups so that they catch the eye and draw it from place to place around the garden, helping to highlight key features. For growing tips, see 'Acropolis' (*page 202*).

OTHER VARIETY *N.* 'Carlton' (soft yellow with a frilled trumpet).

PLANT PROFILE

HEIGHT 16in (40cm)

SPREAD 16cm (6in)

SITE Sun

SOIL Average, moist but free-draining

HARDINESS Z3–9 H9–1

FLOWERING Midspring

Narcissus 'Suzy' Daffodil

N

WITH ONE OR TWO SWEETLY SCENTED FLOWERS per stem, *Narcissus* 'Suzy' has primrose yellow petals and a rich orange cup in the middle. It can be grown in pots and given special treatment to make it flower early indoors, but this really is an elaborate process. Given that bulbs are so easily available and inexpensive, the best thing is to buy them in bud from garden centers, having let the experts do the hard work for you. See 'Acropolis' (*page 202*) for growing tips.

OTHER VARIETY *N.* 'Bobbysoxer' (primrose yellow petals with orange and yellow cups).

PLANT PROFILE
HEIGHT 16in (40cm)
SPREAD 3in (8cm)
SITE Full sun
SOIL Average, moist but free-draining
HARDINESS Z3–9 H9–1
FLOWERING Midspring

N | *Narcissus* 'Sweetness' Daffodil

THE NAME 'SWEETNESS' REFERS to the golden yellow, sweet-scented blooms that open in midspring and make excellent cut flowers. Give it a warm, sheltered site and grow as for *Narcissus* 'Acropolis' (*see page 202*). Like *N. jonquilla* and 'Suzy', 'Sweetness' can be persuaded to flower earlier in pots kept indoors. It is a rather meticulous process, so if you want blooms in the house, buy the bulbs in bud from garden centers.

OTHER VARIETY *N.* 'Quail' (golden yellow flowers).

PLANT PROFILE

HEIGHT 16in (40cm)

SPREAD 3in (8cm)

SITE Full sun

SOIL Average, moist but free-draining

HARDINESS Z3–9 H9–1

FLOWERING Midspring

Narcissus 'Tahiti' Daffodil

'TAHITI' HAS A NICE MIX of rich, golden yellow petals with a dash of bright orange-red in the middle. It also has strong stems, withstands disastrous spring weather quite well, makes an impressive clump on the open lawn, and stands a good chance of winning prizes in local shows. If you have a spare patch of grass or a slope that needs brightening up in the spring, *Narcissus* 'Tahiti' makes a very good choice. Plant extra clumps so that they can be used for cut-flower displays. See 'Acropolis' (*page 202*) for growing tips.

OTHER VARIETY *N.* 'Manly' (soft yellow with tangerine centers).

PLANT PROFILE

HEIGHT 18in (45cm)

SPREAD 6in (15cm)

SITE Sun

SOIL Average, moist but free-draining

HARDINESS Z3–9 H9–1

FLOWERING Midspring

N | *Narcissus* 'Tête-à-Tête' Daffodil

SMALL AND VIGOROUS, *Narcissus* 'Tête-à-Tête' creates attractive clusters of dainty, golden yellow flowers with deeper yellow cups, on strong stems. It can be grown in a wide variety of situations, from lawns with not-too-vigorous grass to pots and narrow strips edging a path. Wherever it is grown, give it a position in the foreground so that it can be clearly seen. A good choice for small gardens. See 'Acropolis' (*page 202*) for growing tips.

OTHER VARIETY *N.* 'Liberty Bells' (clear lemon yellow flowers).

PLANT PROFILE
HEIGHT 6in (15cm)
SPREAD 2in (5cm)
SITE Sun
SOIL Average, moist but free-draining
HARDINESS Z3–9 H9–1
FLOWERING Early spring

Nectaroscordum siculum subsp. *bulgaricum* Honey garlic

THE FLOWERS ARE LIKE DANGLING, downward-pointing, off-white bells, with a green and purple flush, on top of long thin stems. It quickly catches the eye in a garden center, but has more of a supporting part than a lead role in the garden. Although it sounds like a standalone feature plant, it is not quite that interesting and needs to be integrated into a well-designed border to work well. When the flowers fade, they turn parchment brown and can be used in dried flower arrangements. Grow in average, free-draining soil. It self-seeds and produces decent clumps.

OTHER VARIETY *N. siculum* (white or cream flowers flushed pink or purple-red).

PLANT PROFILE	
HEIGHT To 4ft (1.2m)	
SPREAD 4in (10cm)	
SITE Full sun or partial shade	
SOIL Fertile, free-draining	
HARDINESS Z6–10 H10–6	
FLOWERING Midsummer	

N | *Nerine bowdenii* Guernsey lily

EVEN THOUGH IT COMES FROM SOUTH AFRICA, *Nerine bowdenii* is perfectly robust and hardy in some cooler climates. It creates a striking show in autumn when it has faintly scented, pink flowers on top of a stout, upright stem. The leaves appear later, at the start of winter. Plant in early autumn, with the neck of the bulb just showing above the soil, at the foot of a hot, south-facing wall with good drainage. If you live in a frost-prone area, plant it slightly deeper, with a thin, protective covering of soil.

OTHER VARIETY *N. bowdenii* 'Alba' (white flowers, sometimes flushed pale pink).

PLANT PROFILE

HEIGHT 18in (45cm)

SPREAD 3in (8cm)

SITE Full sun

SOIL Average, free-draining

HARDINESS Z8–10 H10–5

FLOWERING Autumn

Nomocharis pardanthina

DESERVING TO BE MUCH MORE POPULAR, this relative of the lily produces 2–20 nodding, initially saucer-shaped, white or pink flowers that then flatten out. They are 2½–3½in (6–9cm) wide and are liberally speckled red-purple, with dark centers, and the petals have fringed tips. Plant the bulbs 6in (15cm) deep in winter or spring, in acidic soil that is rich in organic matter and stays moist, but is never waterlogged, in summer. Avoid hot, dry ground, and look out for slugs.

OTHER VARIETY *N. aperta* (pale pink flowers, spotted deep purple).

PLANT PROFILE	
HEIGHT 3ft (1m)	
SPREAD 4in (10cm)	
SITE Full sun or partial shade	
SOIL Rich in organic matter, moist, acidic	
HARDINESS Z7–9 H9–7	
FLOWERING Early summer	

N | *Notholirion bulbuliferum*

YOU WILL NEED A MILD, SHELTERED, frost-free garden to grow this bulb from western China, because the winter leaves at the base of the plant are easily damaged when the temperature dives. In summer, between 10 and 30 trumpet-shaped, pale lilac flowers with green tips emerge. They are quite small, measuring 1½in (4cm) long. Plant the bulbs 4–6in (10–15 cm) deep in autumn, in soil that is rich in organic matter and free-draining. Partial spring and summer shade is important because it dislikes wall-to-wall sun.

PLANT PROFILE

HEIGHT To 5ft (1.5m)

SPREAD 6in (15cm)

SITE Partial shade

SOIL Rich in organic matter, free-draining

HARDINESS Z7–10

FLOWERING Summer

Nothoscordum inodorum False garlic

THE SOUTH AMERICAN FALSE GARLIC looks a bit like some alliums. Don't be tempted to plant it in a border because it will quickly become a rampant weed, but in wild gardens it is a useful plant to let loose in large areas that need filling. It is a prolific spreader and produces white flowers with a green flush down the middle of the petals over a long period. *Nothoscordum inodorum* needs a mild climate to thrive. Plant the bulbs 3in (7cm) deep in the autumn.

OTHER VARIETY *N. gracile* (white, occasionally lilac flowers).

PLANT PROFILE

HEIGHT 10–28in (25–70cm)

SPREAD 2in (5cm)

SITE Full sun or partial shade

SOIL Average

HARDINESS Z7–9

FLOWERING Spring to summer

O | *Ornithogalum dubium* Star-of-Bethlehem

A SOUTH AFRICAN BULB, *Ornithogalum dubium* is certainly not hardy and needs to be grown in a mild, sheltered, sunny part of the garden. It has large yellow or orange flowers with six flat, open, dark-centered petals. If it is grown in a pot, make sure you add plenty of horticultural sand to a loam-based potting mix to open it up and make it free-draining. Provide water over the winter months and into spring when it starts to flower. This regimen should be followed by a dry, dormant period over summer, but give it an occasional watering or the soil will become too dry.

OTHER VARIETY *O. thyrsoides* (white flowers tinted cream or green at the bases).

PLANT PROFILE

HEIGHT 10–14in (25–35cm)

SPREAD 4in (10cm)

SITE Full sun

SOIL Average, free-draining

HARDINESS Z7–10

FLOWERING Late spring

Ornithogalum narbonense Star-of-Bethlehem

TALLER THAN MOST ORNITHOGALUMS, this one, found growing wild from northern Africa to Turkey and Iran, sends up green stems with clustered buds right toward the top. They open to give a very attractive display of star-shaped white flowers in late spring and, although they won't hog the limelight, they make a decent show between the main spring and summer displays. The leaves are right at the bottom by the soil. Plant bulbs 4in (10cm) deep in average, free-draining soil; although sun is best, it will tolerate partial shade. All parts of the plant may cause severe discomfort if ingested, and the sap may irritate the skin.

OTHER VARIETY *O. umbellatum* (white flowers).

PLANT PROFILE
HEIGHT 12–36in (30–90cm)
SPREAD 2in (5cm)
SITE Full sun
SOIL Average, free-draining
HARDINESS Z7–10 H10–7
FLOWERING Late spring and early summer

O | *Ornithogalum nutans* Star of Bethlehem

AN EASY TO-GROW, cottage garden–type plant with up to 20 small, silver-white flowers with a green stripe in spring. This star-of-Bethlehem can be grown in short grass or around shrubs to follow daffodils. Given ideal conditions, it can become invasive, but is easily controlled by hauling out excess growth. Plant the bulbs 4in (10cm) deep in average, free-draining soil. Sun is best, though it will tolerate partial shade. All parts of the plant may cause severe discomfort if ingested, and the sap may irritate the skin.

PLANT PROFILE

HEIGHT 8–24in (20–60cm)

SPREAD 2in (5cm)

SITE Full sun

SOIL Average, free-draining

HARDINESS Z4–9 H9–5

FLOWERING Spring

Pancratium maritimum Sea daffodil

P

COMING FROM THE MILD COASTLINE of the Mediterranean, the sea daffodil is very tender and best grown in a greenhouse border or in pots for standing outside over summer. There will be up to six scented white flowers, about 4in (10cm) wide. Plant bulbs 6–8in (15–20cm) deep, in pots filled with a loam-based potting mix with added horticultural sand for good drainage. Water freely when in growth, adding liquid fertilizer once a month, and sparingly during autumn and winter. If it is grown outdoors, a sunny, sheltered site with sharp drainage is crucial.

PLANT PROFILE	
HEIGHT 12in (30cm)	
SPREAD 12in (30cm)	
SITE Full sun	
SOIL Average, excellent drainage	
HARDINESS Z8–11	
FLOWERING Late summer	

P

Polianthes tuberosa Tuberose

ONCE ENORMOUSLY POPULAR, *Polianthes tuberosa* deserves to make a comeback because of its exquisite, strongly scented, waxy white summer flowers. Being very tender, it needs to be grown in a pot that can stand outside over summer or be kept in a conservatory. Fill the pot with a loam-based potting mix. Water moderately over summer, adding liquid fertilizer every two weeks. Reduce watering as the leaves die down, and make sure you keep it dry when dormant.

OTHER VARIETY *P. tuberosa* 'The Pearl' (double white flowers).

PLANT PROFILE
HEIGHT To 4ft (1.2m)
SPREAD 6in (15cm)
SITE Full sun
SOIL Average, free-draining
HARDINESS Z7–11 H11–.
FLOWERING Summer

Puschkinia scilloides Striped squill

P

THE PALE BLUE–WHITE FLOWERS of *Puschkinia scilloides* have a tiny cup in the center, and a dark blue stripe on each petal, making a gentle addition to cottage gardens. *P. scilloides* var. *libanotica* (*see inset*) is equally popular, but its smaller white flowers only rarely have blue stripes. Plant the bulbs where there is light summer shade so that they do not bake dry over summer. Congested clumps might need prying out of the ground and dividing every few years before being replanted farther apart to give them more space.

PLANT PROFILE
HEIGHT To 8in (20cm)
SPREAD 2in (5cm)
SITE Full sun or light dappled shade
SOIL Free-draining
HARDINESS Z3–9 H9–1
FLOWERING Spring

R | *Ranunculus asiaticus* Persian buttercup

FORGET TRADITIONAL YELLOW buttercups: *Ranunculus asiaticus* is a rare beauty with five-petaled flowers that are about 1½in (4cm) wide. All have a purple-black center with petals in one of four colors—red, pink, yellow, or white—but the most striking is the white. Being tender, it needs to be grown in a conservatory in pots filled with a loam-based potting mix and added horticultural sand for good drainage. Keep it dry in summer and moist from winter on, when new growth appears, until flowering is finished. Many gardeners stand the pot in a tray filled with water to prevent it from drying out.

PLANT PROFILE

HEIGHT 8–18in (20–45cm)

SPREAD 8in (20cm)

SITE Full sun

SOIL Loam-based potting mix

HARDINESS Z7–11 H12–

FLOWERING Late spring and early summer

Ranunculus bulbosus Bulbous buttercup

R

THE SMALL, RICH, GOLDEN YELLOW FLOWERS of the bulbous buttercup are saucer-shaped and appear at the end of spring. Its height is usually given as 6–16in (15–40cm) but it can sometimes grow up to 32in (80cm) high. It is perfectly easy to grow, and is ideal for borders and rock gardens, though the soil must not be allowed to get too dry. Buttercups are easily overlooked and often regarded as lawn weeds and a thorough nuisance, but they can be quite the reverse, perking things up around the garden. Choose *Ranunculus bulbosus* 'Speciosus Plenus' (*see inset*) for a more elaborate effect.

OTHER VARIETY *R. bulbosus* 'F.M. Burton' (creamy yellow flowers).

PLANT PROFILE	
HEIGHT 16–16in (5–40cm)	
SPREAD 12in (30cm)	
SITE Sun or partial shade	
SOIL Fertile, moist but free-draining	
HARDINESS Z7–9	
FLOWERING Late spring and early summer	

Rhodohypoxis 'Albrighton' Red star

IT MIGHT BE BARELY OVER ANKLE-HEIGHT, but the deep-colored, open, star-shaped, red-pink flowers of *Rhodohypoxis* 'Albrighton' appear all through summer. They stand out smartly against its dull gray-green leaves, which incidentally are very hairy. The only setback is that *R.* 'Albrighton' is rather tender, coming from South Africa, and it definitely needs a sunny, sheltered, free-draining site where it is protected from excessive winter rain. A good bet for the foot of a sunny wall.

OTHER VARIETY *R. baurii* (pale to deep red-pink flowers).

PLANT PROFILE

HEIGHT 4in (10cm)

SPREAD 4in (10cm)

SITE Full sun

SOIL Average, rich in organic matter, free-draining

HARDINESS Z9–10 H10–?

FLOWERING Summer

Rhodophiala advena Oxblood lily

LOOKING A BIT LIKE A HIPPEASTRUM, and once called *H. advena*, *Rhodophiala advena* deserves to be much more popular. It has from two to five trumpet-shaped red, yellow, or pink flowers measuring 2in (5cm) wide on top of long, thin stems. Being tender, it needs to be grown in pots. Fill them with a loam-based potting mix and plant the bulbs in autumn so that their necks and shoulders are just showing above soil level. Water sparingly until in active growth, then moderately, and apply half-strength liquid fertilizer every two to three weeks. Keep dry when dormant. Only move into a larger pot every three years.

OTHER VARIETY *R. bifida* (bright, deep red flowers).

PLANT PROFILE

HEIGHT 6–12in (15–30cm)

SPREAD 12–20in (30–50cm)

SITE Full sun

SOIL Loam-based potting mix

HARDINESS Z9–10 H10–9

FLOWERING Late summer and early autumn

R | *Romulea bulbocodium* Sand crocus

THE PALE TO DEEP LILAC PURPLE FLOWERS of *Romulea bulbocodium* are funnel-shaped and 1in (2.5cm) long, with a white or yellow center. Being small, slightly tender, and in need of free-draining soil, it can be grown in sheltered, sunny rock gardens or at the foot of a warm wall. The most important thing is to ensure that the plant is kept completely dry over summer when dormant. If that proves tricky, grow it in a pot filled with a loam-based potting mix with added sand for fast drainage. Water moderately in the growing season, and apply a monthly liquid feeding. After flowering, reduce the water gradually.

OTHER VARIETY *R. nivalis* (lilac to mauve flowers; yellow within).

PLANT PROFILE

HEIGHT 2–4in (5–10cm)

SPREAD 2in (5cm)

SITE Full sun

SOIL Average, free-draining

HARDINESS Z5–9 H9–5

FLOWERING Spring

Roscoea cautleyoides

AN INTRIGUING MEMBER of the ginger family from the Far East, *Roscoea cautleyoides* has 1⅛in- (4cm-) wide yellow, white, or purple flowers. They catch the eye right at the start of summer when there is little competition from other plants, and even its own leaves have not fully unfurled. Plant it at the front of a border where it can be clearly seen. *R. cautleyoides* prefers rich, leafy soil in a cool, sheltered site. If there is any likelihood of frost, apply a protective, thick winter mulch to insulate the roots.

OTHER VARIETY *R. auriculata* (*see page 258*).

PLANT PROFILE
HEIGHT To 22in (55cm)
SPREAD 6in (15cm)
SITE Partial shade
SOIL Rich in organic matter, leafy, moist but free-draining
HARDINESS Z6–9 H9–6
FLOWERING Early summer

R | *Roscoea auriculata*

A GOOD CHOICE FOR ITS LATE-SEASON DISPLAY, *Roscoea auriculata* (once known as *R. purpurea* var. *auriculata*) has showy purple flowers that open in sequence, one after the other. In the wild it is found in India and the Himalayas, and in parts of North America it just needs a cool, sheltered part of the border. If there is any likelihood of frost, apply a thick, protective winter mulch to help insulate the roots. It belongs to the ginger family, and other good alternatives include *R. purpurea*, which has large, lavender purple flowers, and its new forms *R. purpurea* 'Polaris', with short red stems and near-white flowers, and the large flowered, lavender-purple *R. purpurea* 'Nico'.

OTHER VARIETY *R. auriculata* 'Floriade' (intense violet flowers).

PLANT PROFILE

HEIGHT 10–16in (25–40cm)

SPREAD 6in (15cm)

SITE Partial shade

SOIL Fertile, leafy, moist but free-draining

HARDINESS Z6–9

FLOWERING Late summer

Scadoxus multiflorus Blood lily

S

A TROPICAL SOUTH AFRICAN PLANT (sometimes still known as *Haemanthus multiflorus*), the blood lily has 4–6in (10–15cm) heads consisting of up to 200 tiny red flowers followed by small orange berries. To grow one, plant the bulb in a pot filled with a loam-based potting mix in autumn or winter, leaving the neck at soil level. Keep it in bright light, shading it from full sun. Then, as the buds open, place it in partial shade. Water freely when in full growth, and apply a half-strength liquid fertilizer every month. As the leaves fade, reduce watering, and keep dry when dormant. A good alternative is *Scadoxus multiflorus* subsp. *katherinae*, which looks similar but has wavy-margined leaves (*see inset*).

PLANT PROFILE

HEIGHT To 24in (60cm)

SPREAD 6in (15cm)

SITE Bright light or light, dappled shade

SOIL Rich in organic matter, moist but free-draining

HARDINESS Z14–15 H12–10

FLOWERING Summer

S | *Scilla peruviana* 'Alba' White Peruvian squill

THE LARGE MEDITERRANEAN BULBS, which actually have no connection with Peru, produce showy clusters of 50–100 small, starlike white flowers with a yellow eye, packed together at the top of a stem. *Scilla peruviana* 'Alba' makes a novel sight in early summer. The lush, swordlike leaves precede the flowers by months, appearing in the autumn. Plant bulbs 3–4in (8–10cm) deep in late summer or early autumn in free-draining soil. A sunny position is essential; keep them out of the shade.

OTHER VARIETY *S. bithynica* (star-shaped, blue flowers).

PLANT PROFILE
HEIGHT 6–12in (15–30cm)
SPREAD 4in (10cm)
SITE Full sun or partial shade
SOIL Average, rich in organic matter, free-draining
HARDINESS Z8–9 H9–8
FLOWERING Early summer

Scilla siberica 'Spring Beauty' Siberian squill

S

SIBERIAN SQUILL IS A SMALL PLANT with just two to four short leaves, making it a good choice for an early summer show in rock gardens, right at the front of a border, or in gaps in patio paving. 'Spring Beauty' is chiefly grown for its deep blue, dangling flowers which appear in loose clusters, and can be mixed in small clumps with the white *S. siberica* 'Alba' and bright blue *S. siberica* to give a colorful show. All scillas can be grown through violets, and the darker blue or pink ones also look good in combination with grape hyacinths. See *S. peruviana* 'Alba' (*opposite*) for growing tips.

OTHER VARIETY *S. siberica* 'Alba' (white flowers).

PLANT PROFILE
HEIGHT To 8in (20cm)
SPREAD 2in (5cm)
SITE Full sun or partial shade
SOIL Average, rich in organic matter, free-draining
HARDINESS Z5–8 H8–5
FLOWERING Spring

S

Sparaxis tricolor Harlequin flower

A TENDER SOUTH AFRICAN, this harlequin flower has a fan of erect, 12in- (30cm-) long leaves, and up to five stems carrying between two and five funnel-shaped orange, red, or yellow flowers. Each one is about 2½in (6.5cm) wide with a dark central mark. In the wild it makes a flashy spread, but in cooler regions it needs to be grown in conservatory pots. Plant it 4in (10cm) deep in a loam-based potting mix with added leaf mold and horticultural sand for sharp drainage. Water sparingly in growth and place it out of direct sun in the garden. Reduce watering as the flowers fade, and keep dry in the conservatory when dormant.

PLANT PROFILE

HEIGHT 4–16in (10–40cm)

SPREAD 3in (8cm)

SITE Full sun

SOIL Loam-based potting mix

HARDINESS Z7–10 H10–7

FLOWERING Spring to early summer

Sprekelia formosissima Aztec lily

S

THE FANTASTICALLY FLASHY and beautiful scarlet to crimson flowers of the Aztec lily are found on rocky slopes in Mexico and Guatemala. The bulbs are well worth growing in pots filled with a fertile, loam-based potting mix. Plant them in the autumn, leaving the neck and shoulder above soil level. When in growth, water moderately and apply half-strength liquid fertilizer every two weeks after flowering. As the foliage fades, reduce watering, and keep dry when dormant. Repot every two to three years, but no more because it hates having its roots disturbed.

PLANT PROFILE
HEIGHT 6–14in (15–35cm)
SPREAD 6in (15cm)
SITE Full sun
SOIL Fertile, loam-based potting mix
HARDINESS Z13–15 H12–10
FLOWERING Spring

S | *Sternbergia lutea* Autumn daffodil

MORE OF A YELLOW AUTUMN CROCUS than a daffodil, the short *Sternbergia lutea* is certainly flashy with its rich yellow, gobletlike flowers. They are nicely set off by the dark green leaves, but if possible, you should also provide a dark green background. Because *S. lutea* also needs sharply drained soil in a sunny position, it is traditionally grown at the foot of a hedge, where large clumps soon appear. Plant bulbs 6in (15cm) deep in late summer. If flowering starts to decline, lift the congested clump and replant sections farther apart.

OTHER VARIETY *S. clusiana* (yellow flowers).

PLANT PROFILE
HEIGHT 6in (15cm)
SPREAD 3in (8cm)
SITE Full sun
SOIL Average, excellent drainage
HARDINESS Z7–9 H9–6
FLOWERING Autumn

Tecophilaea cyanocrocus Chilean blue crocus

T

THE FLOWERS ARE A STARTLING, VIVID BLUE, and although the Chilean blue crocus is not totally hardy, it is worth trying if you have a frost-free part of the garden. Fast drainage and summer drought are important, which means that your options are rock gardens and raised beds with sandy soil, or greenhouse pots filled with a loam-based potting mix and added horticultural sand. Water moderately when growing, then reduce the amount as the leaves fade, and keep warm over summer.

OTHER VARIETY *T. cyanocrocus* 'Leichtlinii' (pale blue flowers with large white centers).

PLANT PROFILE	
HEIGHT 3–4in (8–10cm)	
SPREAD 2in (5cm)	
SITE Full sun	
SOIL Free-draining, sandy	
HARDINESS Z7–9 H9–7	
FLOWERING Spring	

T

Tigridia pavonia Tiger flower

THE 4–6IN- (10–15CM-) WIDE, exotic orange to pink, red, yellow, or white flowers of the tiger flower might last just a few hours, but they are spectacular, and successive buds keep appearing over summer. Too tender to be grown outside, except in the mildest areas, they can be grown in a conservatory border or pot. In conservatories the soil needs to be sandy and free-draining; outside, bulbs can be lifted after flowering and protected over winter in dry sand at 50°F (10°C). Pots should be filled with a loam-based potting mix and additional horticultural sand. Water freely in growth, and keep dry when dormant. Repot them each spring.

OTHER VARIETY *T. pavonia* 'Aurea' (yellow and red flowers).

PLANT PROFILE
HEIGHT 5ft (1.5m)
SPREAD 4in (10cm)
SITE Full sun
SOIL Fertile, sandy, free-draining
HARDINESS Z8–10 H12–3
FLOWERING Summer

Triteleia hyacinthina White brodiaea

THE WHITE OR PALE BLUE FLOWERING BULBS of *Triteleia hyacinthina* add a gentle touch to cottage gardens between spring and summer. Clusters of about 20 tiny flowers appear on upright stems, with the dormant period following in the summer. The soil needs to be light and free-draining in a sheltered, sunny position. In frost-prone areas, bulbs can be grown in pots filled with loam-based potting mix and added horticultural sand. Water sparingly until the leaves appear, and freely when in growth, adding half-strength liquid fertilizer every month. After flowering, reduce watering, and keep dry when dormant.

OTHER VARIETY *T. ixioides* (yellow flowers with purple midribs).

PLANT PROFILE
HEIGHT To 28in (70cm)
SPREAD 2in (5cm)
SITE Full sun
SOIL Light, sandy, fertile
HARDINESS Z7–13 H12–7
FLOWERING Late spring and early summer

T | *Triteleia laxa* Ithuriel's spear

RIGHT AT THE START OF SUMMER the deep purple-blue coloring of *Triteleia laxa* makes quite an eye-catching sight. Some plants have white flowers, but this is rare. If you like *T. hyacinthina* (*see page 267*), *T. laxa* will take over as it starts to fade, adding an informal touch in cottage gardens. *T. laxa* is not hardy, and may need to be grown in pots filled with a loam-based potting mix for standing outside when it flowers. Keep it in a greenhouse to guarantee the essential warmth and dryness while the bulb is dormant. For growing tips, see *T. hyacinthina*.

OTHER VARIETY *T. laxa* 'Koningin Fabiola' (purple-blue flowers).

PLANT PROFILE	
HEIGHT To 28in (70cm)	
SPREAD 2in (5cm)	
SITE Full sun	
SOIL Light, sandy, fertile	
HARDINESS Z6–10 H10–6	
FLOWERING Early summer	

Tritonia disticha subsp. *rubrolucens* Blazing star

T

THIS SOUTH AFRICAN BULB has a succession of small pink blooms that angle through its leaves on thin, wiry stems. It flowers only briefly in early summer, but it does spread well, making decent clumps; create extra plants by dividing them in spring. Plant the bulbs 4in (10cm) deep. Make sure the ground is free-draining and on the dry side over winter; this often means a sunny, sheltered position at the foot of a wall. *Tritonia disticha* subsp. *rubrolucens* also needs a protective, thick winter mulch. It might be easier to grow in pots filled with a loam-based potting mix and plenty of added sharp sand; keep fairly dry when dormant.

OTHER VARIETY *T. disticha* (flowers in red, orange-red, or pink).

PLANT PROFILE

HEIGHT 20in (50cm)

SPREAD 2in (5cm)

SITE Full sun

SOIL Light, sandy, free-draining

HARDINESS Z9–10 H10–9

FLOWERING Early summer

T

Tulipa 'Aladdin' Tulip

A BOLD, VIVID, GOBLET-SHAPED TULIP, *Tulipa* 'Aladdin' has contrasting yellow margins around the scarlet flowers, and stands out a few weeks before the start of summer. Plant the bulbs 4in (10cm) deep in free-draining soil. Promptly cut off the fading petals, but allow the foliage to die down naturally. Dig up the bulbs when the leaves have been removed, and store in a cool, dry place for replanting in late autumn (no earlier, in case premature spring growth gets caught by a frost) or early winter. Bulbs probably need replacing after three years. Grow 'Aladdin' in large, bold blocks with other tulips, or let it swirl in packs through a border.

OTHER VARIETY *T.* 'Ballade' (white-margined, red-magenta flowers).

PLANT PROFILE
HEIGHT 18in (45cm)
SITE Full sun
SOIL Fertile, free-draining
HARDINESS Z3–8 H8–1
FLOWERING Late spring

Tulipa 'Angélique' **Tulip**

T

THE FLOWERS ARE A BEAUTIFUL MIX of pale pink flushed with other shades of pink, and turn slightly darker as they age. Occasionally there is a green or yellow base. Exquisite and subtle, it is a good choice particularly if you dislike the in-your-face kind of tulips in bright reds and yellows. Grow 'Angélique' to highlight and embellish specific parts of the garden, drawing the eye to statues, colorful urns, or strong geometric shapes. For growing tips, see 'Aladdin' (*opposite*).

PLANT PROFILE
HEIGHT 12in (30cm)
SITE Full sun
SOIL Fertile, free-draining
HARDINESS Z3–8 H8–1
FLOWERING Midspring

OTHER VARIETY *T.* 'Carnaval de Nice' (*see page 280*).

T

Tulipa 'Apeldoorn' Tulip

THE LARGE FLOWERS are flashy cherry red with black edging on the inside, and added yellow marks. *Tulipa* 'Apeldoorn' stands out nicely against groups of white and yellow tulips, and with its strong, eye-catching color can be used to draw the eye toward key features in the garden and away from others. The red can also be used to contrast with white-stemmed trees, such as the Himalayan birch (*Betula utilis* var. *jacquemontii*). 'Apeldoorn' also makes good cut flowers. Grow as for 'Aladdin' (*see page 270*).

OTHER VARIETY *T.* 'Jewel of Spring' (red-margined, sulfur yellow flowers with green-black bases and black anthers).

PLANT PROFILE	
HEIGHT	24in (60cm)
SITE	Full sun
SOIL	Fertile, free-draining
HARDINESS	Z3–8 H8–1
FLOWERING	Midspring

Tulipa 'Apricot Beauty' Tulip

THE UNUSUAL COLOR is soft salmon-pink, slightly darker on the inside. See *Tulipa* 'Aladdin' (*page 270*) for growing tips. 'Apricot Beauty' is a member of the Single Early Group of tulips, and can also be grown in pots for flowering at the end of winter. To do this, plant the bulbs in early or midautumn in pots filled with a loam-based potting mix, with the tip of the bulb just showing. Keep in a cool, dark place at a maximum of 45°F (7°C) until the leaf tips show, then bring indoors or into a greenhouse at 50°F (10°C). When the leaves reach 4in (10cm) long, gradually raise the temperature to a maximum of 64°F (18°C).

OTHER VARIETY *T.* 'Van der Neer' (plum purple, sometimes with white feathering).

PLANT PROFILE	
HEIGHT 14in (35cm)	
SITE Full sun	
SOIL Fertile, free-draining	
HARDINESS Z3–8 H8–1	
FLOWERING Midspring	

T | *Tulipa* 'Artist' **Tulip**

THE LATE-SPRING, PALE TERRACOTTA FLOWERS of *Tulipa* 'Artist' have broad green stripes on the outside, and are salmon-pink with a green flush inside. Avoid planting them against the foot of a red brick wall because they will immediately lose their impact. 'Artist' is often listed with the Viridiflora tulips in bulb catalogs. Many of the others also have green stripes—for example, the lovely white 'Spring Green' and apricot 'Green River'—and all flower at the end of spring. For growing tips, see 'Aladdin' (*page 270*).

OTHER VARIETY *T.* 'Esperanto' (pink-red flowers with green veins and yellow-brown anthers).

PLANT PROFILE	
HEIGHT 18in (45cm)	
SITE Full sun	
SOIL Fertile, free-draining	
HARDINESS Z3–8 H8–1	
FLOWERING Late spring	

Tulipa 'Attila' Tulip

T

THE STRONG STEMS of *Tulipa* 'Attila' carry light purple violet flowers, making it a useful addition to a group of richly colored tulips, and for adding zest to groups of paler colors. 'Attila' is also very good for growing in pots to flower early indoors; plant them in early to midautumn in loam–based potting mix, with the tips of the bulbs just showing. Keep in a cool, dark place for six weeks until the leaf tips show, then place in a room at 50°F (10°C). When the leaves are 4in (10cm) long, increase the temperature to a maximum of 64°F (18°C).

OTHER VARIETY *T.* 'Arabian Mystery' (dark purple flowers with white margins).

PLANT PROFILE	
HEIGHT	16in (40cm)
SITE	Full sun
SOIL	Fertile, free-draining
HARDINESS	Z3–8 H8–1
FLOWERING	Midspring

T | *Tulipa aucheriana* Tulip

THE 6IN- (15CM-) LONG, glossy leaves of *Tulipa aucheriana* can engulf its low growing, star-shaped, pink flowers with yellow in the center. *T. aucheriana* can be grown in rock gardens or at the foot of a sunny wall. Provided there is free-draining soil, it can be safely left in the ground all year, and does not need to be dug up and dried over summer; otherwise, grow as for 'Aladdin' (*page 270*).

OTHER VARIETY *T. pulchella* (light crimson or purple flowers with blue-black marks at the base).

PLANT PROFILE

HEIGHT 4–10in (10–25cm)

SITE Full sun

SOIL Fertile, free-draining

HARDINESS Z3–8 H8–1

FLOWERING Midspring

Tulipa 'Ballerina' Tulip

T

A FLAMBOYANT, BEAUTIFULLY SHAPED TULIP, 'Ballerina' is often described as being flame red against a lemon yellow background, with orange-yellow veining. Inside it is red with marigold orange feathering. 'Ballerina' is a good choice for a bright color scheme that will end the spring with a bang. Use it in large, bold groups, and to create a strong contrast with paler-colored tulips. See 'Aladdin' (*page 270*) for growing tips.

PLANT PROFILE	
HEIGHT 24in (60cm)	
SITE Full sun	
SOIL Fertile, free-draining	
HARDINESS Z3–8 H8–1	
FLOWERING Late spring	

OTHER VARIETY *T.* 'Queen of Sheba' (brown-red flowers with orange margins).

T

Tulipa biflora Tulip

THE TINY, STAR-SHAPED, scented white flowers of *Tulipa biflora* do not look anything like the big, brash tulips found in public parks. They are yellow at the base, and the backs of the petals have a touch of green with violet-gray that gradually darkens. In the wild, it grows in Afghanistan and eastern Turkey in rocky, stony ground that is extremely free-draining. It needs similar fast-draining sites in the garden, where it can be left all year; otherwise, grow as for 'Aladdin' (*see page 270*).

OTHER VARIETY *T. bifloriformis* (creamy white flowers with creamy yellow at the base).

PLANT PROFILE

HEIGHT 4in (10cm)

SITE Full sun

SOIL Average, excellent drainage

HARDINESS Z3–8 H8–1

FLOWERING Late winter to spring

Tulipa 'Blue Parrot' Tulip

T

A LARGE TULIP, it has brightly colored flowers that are a lovely violet-blue and bronze-purple inside. It mixes well with most tulips, though it is also worth growing around trees with pale gray or white trunks, such as *Betula utilis* var. *jacquemontii*. It is known as a "parrot" because it belongs to the Parrot Group, which includes some outrageous colors, much more extroverted than this, like the yellow and red 'Flaming Parrot'. See 'Aladdin' (*page 270*) for growing tips.

OTHER VARIETY *T.* 'Rococo' (carmine red, margined fire red).

PLANT PROFILE	
HEIGHT 24in (60cm)	
SITE Full sun	
SOIL Fertile, free-draining	
HARDINESS Z3–8 H8–1	
FLOWERING Late spring	

T

Tulipa 'Carnaval de Nice' Tulip

A SHOWY, FUN TULIP that is more respectable than vulgar,
T. 'Carnaval de Nice' has white, cup-shaped flowers with dark
raspberry red marks and is worth growing to brighten up the
garden. Use it to contrast with clumps of yellow or mauve
tulips, to stand out against shrubs with glossy, evergreen foliage,
such as *Choisya ternata*, or ornamental trees with dark brown or
greenish trunks, and to puncture the myth that tulips have to be
exquisitely elegant. See 'Aladdin' (*page 270*) for growing tips.

PLANT PROFILE
HEIGHT 16in (40cm)
SITE Full sun
SOIL Fertile, free-draining
HARDINESS Z3–8 H8–1
FLOWERING Late spring

OTHER VARIETY T. 'Maywonder' (rose pink flowers).

Tulipa 'China Pink' Tulip

T

A BEAUTIFUL, ELEGANT TULIP, 'China Pink' has stylish, pointed buds
and a soft pink color. It is good for toning down tulips with bolder,
richer colors, and for introducing a subtle note to parts of the
garden where style and restraint are the key virtues. It stands out
best against a dark green rather than a white background and is
highly rated by all the experts. Grow as for 'Aladdin' (*see page 270*).

PLANT PROFILE
HEIGHT 20in (50cm)
SITE Full sun
SOIL Fertile, free-draining
HARDINESS Z3–8 H8–1
FLOWERING Late spring

OTHER VARIETY *T.* 'White Triumphator' (white flowers with a
hint of green).

T

Tulipa 'Estella Rijnveld' **Tulip**

A FUN, ZANY, red and white tulip, which looks like a blob of raspberry ripple ice cream, though it might be too garish for some. Give it strongly colored or relatively anonymous companion plants, but nothing too stylish. What it lacks in humility and elegance it makes up for with its boisterous ego. For growing tips, see 'Aladdin' (*page 270*). 'Apricot Parrot' offers a similar shape in a different color.

OTHER VARIETY *T.* 'Texas Gold' (red-margined, bright golden-yellow flowers).

PLANT PROFILE	
HEIGHT 22in (55cm)	
SITE Full sun	
SOIL Fertile, free-draining	
HARDINESS Z3–8 H8–1	
FLOWERING Late spring	

Tulipa 'Generaal de Wet' Tulip

T

THE GOLDEN-ORANGE FLOWERS of *Tulipa* 'Generaal de Wet' have dark orange shading. A strong contender for a lively midspring show, it adds an extra hue to the more obvious reds and yellows. If you stick your nose right in on a hot sunny day, you may just detect a scent. The "Generaal" of its name is a reference to the South African Boer War (1899–1902). It is one of the Single Early Tulips, and may be grown in pots to flowers earlier, at the end of winter. See 'Apricot Beauty' (*page 273*) for growing tips.

PLANT PROFILE	
HEIGHT	16in (40cm)
SITE	Full sun
SOIL	Fertile, free-draining
HARDINESS	Z3–8 H8–1
FLOWERING	Midspring

T | *Tulipa* 'Giuseppe Verdi' Tulip

'GIUSEPPE VERDI' HAS CARMINE RED FLOWERS with a yellow edge, while inside it is golden yellow with red marks. It belongs to the Kaufmanniana Group, which includes small tulips, generally 6–12in (15–30cm) high, that are good ingredients for rock gardens, positions at the front of a border, or gaps in patio paving. For growing tips, see 'Aladdin' (*page 270*), but note that 'Giuseppe Verdi' can be left in the ground for several years and does not need to be stored over summer.

OTHER VARIETY *T.* 'Ancilla' (soft pink flowers with a rose red flush).

PLANT PROFILE	
HEIGHT 8in (20cm)	
SITE Full sun	
SOIL Fertile, free-draining	
HARDINESS Z3–8 H8–1	
FLOWERING Midspring	

Tulipa 'Golden Apeldoorn' Tulip

T

SUNNY AND BRASH, *Tulipa* 'Golden Apeldoorn' is a reliable eye-catcher in midspring, when its golden yellow flowers are carried on strong stems. Inside each, there is a star-shaped black base with bronze-green edging. Grow 'Golden Apeldoorn' with blue, red, and white tulips to create a multicolored look, though you will need to plan the combinations in advance to keep the colors from looking too chaotically jumbled. Alternatively, just grow them in clumps to take over from an early show of daffodils. See 'Aladdin' (*page 270*) for growing tips.

PLANT PROFILE	
HEIGHT 24in (60cm)	
SITE Full sun	
SOIL Fertile, free-draining	
HARDINESS Z3–8 H8–1	
FLOWERING Midspring	

T | *Tulipa hageri* 'Splendens' Tulip

THE STAR-SHAPED PARENT of *Tulipa hageri* 'Splendens' grows in the eastern Mediterranean in Greece and Turkey. It has given rise to this very attractive and popular bright red tulip that is brown-red inside. 'Splendens' needs a free-draining hot spot in the garden and can be succesfully left out all year, but without these conditions it will need to be dug up for the summer; grow as for 'Aladdin' (*see page 270*).

OTHER VARIETY *T. hageri* (green-tinged, dull red with black inside).

PLANT PROFILE

HEIGHT 14in (35cm)

SITE Full sun

SOIL Fertile, free-draining

HARDINESS Z3–8 H8–1

FLOWERING Early and midspring

Tulipa humilis Violacea Group Tulip

T

THE STAR-SHAPED, PURPLE FLOWERS of the short *Tulipa humilis*
are pale pink to purple-pink or magenta, and grow on rocky slopes
and thin grass near the snowline around Iraq and Iran. The related
Violacea Group is purple with a yellow or dark center (*see inset*),
and has similar leaves that are gray-green and 6in (15cm) long.
They both need full sun and excellent drainage, such as in a rock
garden, and can be left out all year. Otherwise, see the growing
tips for 'Aladdin' (*page 270*).

PLANT PROFILE	
HEIGHT To 10in (25cm)	
SITE Full sun	
SOIL Fertile, free-draining	
HARDINESS Z3–8 H8–1	
FLOWERING Early and midspring	

OTHER VARIETY *T. humilis* 'Eastern Star' (rose-colored flowers with
a yellow base and a dash of bronze-green outside).

T | *Tulipa* 'Kees Nelis' Tulip

A RICH BLOOD RED, *Tulipa* 'Kees Nelis' is edged with orange-yellow, making an eye-catching focal point in midspring. It is the highlight in any group of quieter pastel colors, although it can also be used in a lively mix with whites, yellows, and blues. It is an excellent tulip for drawing the eye straight to a key part of the garden where there are strong architectural features. Grow as for 'Aladdin' (*see page 270*).

OTHER VARIETY *T.* 'African Queen' (dark purple-red flowers, with purple-margined, primrose yellow marks at the base).

PLANT PROFILE	
HEIGHT 16in (40cm)	
SITE Full sun	
SOIL Fertile, free-draining	
HARDINESS Z3–8 H8–1	
FLOWERING Midspring	

Tulipa 'Keizerskroon' Tulip

T

VERY POPULAR SINCE THE 18TH CENTURY, *Tulipa* 'Keizerskroon' is a tall, flamboyant, scarlet and yellow tulip with a great big ego that needs careful handling. Although the yellow appears around the edge, both colors are equally dominant. Wherever it is placed in the garden, it is an attention-grabber, so use it to guide the eye to the strongest parts of the garden's design and keep it away from eyesores. For growing tips, see 'Aladdin' (*page 270*).

PLANT PROFILE
HEIGHT 12in (30cm)
SITE Full sun
SOIL Fertile, free-draining
HARDINESS Z3–8 H8–1
FLOWERING Midspring

OTHER VARIETY *T.* 'Brilliant Star' (bright vermilion flowers).

T | *Tulipa linifolia* Batalinii Group Tulip

IDEAL FOR ROCK OR GRAVEL GARDENS, or growing in short grass, these short red, yellow, apricot, and bronze tulips can be left in the ground without any need for you to lift the bulbs and dry them over summer. One of the best in the group is 'Red Jewel', which is scarlet inside with a pink flush outside. The parent *Tulipa linifolia* has scarlet red flowers with a black-purple base (*see inset*). If it is going to be left outside all year, the soil must be very free-draining; otherwise, see the growing tips for 'Aladdin' (*page 270*).

OTHER VARIETY *T. clusiana* 'Cynthia' (creamy yellow flowers with a red tinge outside).

PLANT PROFILE

HEIGHT 6in (15cm)

SITE Full sun

SOIL Fertile, free-draining

HARDINESS Z3–8 H8–1

FLOWERING Early and midspring

Tulipa 'Madame Lefeber' Tulip

T

BELONGING TO THE FOSTERIANA HYBRID GROUP, *Tulipa* 'Madame Lefeber' has two big selling points. First, it flowers earlier than most of the other Fosterianas, which generally do not open until midspring. Second, it has bold red petals that are typical of the rich colors that characterize the group. Plant the bulbs against white walls or trees with white trunks to create a sharp contrast, and at the front of statues to add a flash of color. It also makes a nice combination with small daffodils. For growing tips see 'Aladdin' (*page 270*). 'Cantata' has a similar shape but is a different color.

OTHER VARIETY *T.* 'Orange Emperor' (flashy bright orange with a soft yellow base).

PLANT PROFILE

HEIGHT 16in (40cm)

SITE Full sun

SOIL Fertile, free-draining

HARDINESS Z3–8 H8–1

FLOWERING Early spring

T | *Tulipa* 'Marilyn' Tulip

THE ELEGANT, STYLISH, goblet-shaped flowers of *Tulipa* 'Marilyn' are predominantly creamy white in color with some blood red at the tips and base. It has good garden presence, and is particularly attractive planted toward the front of topiarized evergreens, where it adds a formal touch. 'Marilyn' belongs to the Lily-flowered Group of tulips, which is where you will often find it listed in bulb catalogs. For growing tips, see 'Aladdin' (*page 270*).

OTHER VARIETY *T.* 'Mariette' (rose pink with white bases inside).

PLANT PROFILE

HEIGHT 22in (55cm)

SITE Full sun

SOIL Fertile, free-draining

HARDINESS Z3–8 H8–1

FLOWERING Late spring

Tulipa marjolletii Tulip

FOUND GROWING WILD in southeastern France, *Tulipa marjolletii* has beautiful coloring with pink edging around the creamy white petals, and a slight light purple flush on the outside. Inside, each petal has a green stripe. It is not commonly available, but can be tracked down from specialist bulb suppliers. Given free–draining soil, it can be left outside all year without any ill effects, but if that cannot be provided, see the growing tips for 'Aladdin' (*page 270*).

PLANT PROFILE
HEIGHT 18in (45cm)
SITE Full sun
SOIL Fertile, free-draining
HARDINESS Z3–8 H8–1
FLOWERING Early and midspring

T | *Tulipa* 'Monte Carlo' Tulip

THE SULFUR YELLOW FLOWERS of *Tulipa* 'Monte Carlo' are rich
gold inside and slightly paler on the outside, with a hint of red
feathering. It makes a good cut flower, and if you get your nose in
close, it is possible to detect a faint scent. In catalogs 'Monte Carlo'
is often listed with the Double Early Group, which flowers
in midspring. For growing tips, see 'Aladdin' (*page 270*).

OTHER VARIETY *T.* 'Fringed Beauty' (vermilion flowers with golden
yellow fringes).

PLANT PROFILE

HEIGHT 12in (30cm)

SITE Full sun

SOIL Fertile, free-draining

HARDINESS Z3–8 H8–1

FLOWERING Midspring

Tulipa 'New Design' Tulip

T

THE PALE YELLOW FLOWERS of *Tulipa* 'New Design' fade to pink-white on the outside, and have a red edge. Inside, there is a dash of apricot with a butter yellow base. To add to the subtle mix of tones, the leaves have pink-white margins. A good choice for anyone who does not want too many shrieking yellows in the garden. It can also be used in the foreground, leading to a group of bolder-colored tulips. See 'Aladdin' (*page 270*) for growing tips.

OTHER VARIETY *T.* 'Garden Party' (white flowers, carmine red at the margins, insides are feathered carmine red with red bases).

PLANT PROFILE	
HEIGHT 18in (45cm)	
SITE Full sun	
SOIL Fertile, free-draining	
HARDINESS Z3–8 H8–1	
FLOWERING Midspring	

T

Tulipa orphanidea Orange wild tulip

THE OUTSIDE COLOR of *Tulipa orphanidea* is buff, usually with a green tinge, while the inside varies from brick red to buff with a dark mark at the base. In the wild it can be found growing in fields and on hot rocky sites in Greece and western Turkey. If *T. orphanidea* is to be left outside in the garden all year in cool-climate areas, the soil must be free-draining, as in a gravel or Mediterranean-style garden, because it hates standing in cold, wet ground. If these conditions cannot be provided, see the growing tips for 'Aladdin' (*page 270*).

OTHER VARIETY *T. orphanidea* 'Flava' (yellow flowers with a red flush on the back of the petals).

PLANT PROFILE

HEIGHT 14in (35cm)

SITE Full sun

SOIL Fertile, free-draining

HARDINESS Z3–8 H8–1

FLOWERING Mid- and late spring

Tulipa 'Peach Blossom' Tulip

T

FORGET THE PEACH REFERENCE in the name, because the color is actually a mix of two hues: silver-pink and rose pink. Reactions to it vary. Some experts sniff and mutter about its shape because it lacks the crisp outline of many tulips, while the specialist bulb catalogs rave about its color. There is no doubt, however, that it is a lovely choice for cottage gardens. For growing tips, see 'Aladdin' (*page 270*).

PLANT PROFILE
HEIGHT 12in (30cm)
SITE Full sun
SOIL Fertile, free-draining
HARDINESS Z3–8 H8–1
FLOWERING Midspring

OTHER VARIETY *T.* 'Oranje Nassau' (blood red, flushed fire red).

T

Tulipa praestans 'Unicum' Tulip

AN UNUSUAL TULIP because it has attractively colored leaves with creamy white margins, as well as delightful bright red flowers with light yellow at the base (*see inset*). *Tulipa praestans* 'Unicum' is well worth including in a collection of more obvious, big-name tulips, and is a good contender for cottage gardens. Given free-draining soil, 'Unicum' can be left outside all year without any need for you to dig up the bulbs and keep them dry over summer. Grow as for 'Aladdin' (*see page 270*).

OTHER VARIETY *T. praestans* 'Fusilier' (bright red flowers).

PLANT PROFILE

HEIGHT 12in (30cm)

SITE Full sun

SOIL Fertile, free-draining

HARDINESS Z3–8 H8–1

FLOWERING Early and midspring

Tulipa praestans 'Van Tubergen's Variety' Tulip

INTRODUCTION IN 1914, *Tulipa praestans* 'Van Tubergen's Variety' is an old variety that injects plenty of spark into tired gardens. It has bold, bright, orange-scarlet flowers, but place it with care if you want to avoid visual overkill. Given free-draining soil, it can be successfully left outside all year without any need for you to dig up the bulbs and keep them dry over summer. Otherwise, see 'Aladdin' (*page 270*) for growing tips.

PLANT PROFILE
HEIGHT 20in (50cm)
SITE Full sun
SOIL Fertile, free-draining
HARDINESS Z3–8 H8–1
FLOWERING Early and midspring

OTHER VARIETY *T.* 'Alfred Cortot' (deep scarlet with a black base).

T

Tulipa 'Prinses Irene' Tulip

A HIGHLY RATED and very attractive, unusual tulip, 'Prinses Irene' features a mix of various shades. The petals are quiet orange with a dash of purple and just a hint of green. Inside, they are orange with yellow at the base. 'Prinses Irene' is a good choice for a wide range of gardens, whether they are exquisitely stylish or a more free-and-easy cottage garden. For growing tips see 'Aladdin' (*page 270*).

PLANT PROFILE	
HEIGHT 14in (35cm)	
SITE Full sun	
SOIL Fertile, free-draining	
HARDINESS Z3–8 H8–1	
FLOWERING Midspring	

OTHER VARIETY *T.* 'Palestrina' (salmon-pink tinged green outside).

Tulipa 'Purissima' Tulip

T

THE LARGE, PURE WHITE FLOWERS of *Tulipa* 'Purissima' open on strong stems, and the leaves are gray-green. It belongs to a group called the Fosteriana Hybrids, characterized by their rich coloring, most of which flower at about the same time. 'Purissima' gets all-white gardens off to a good start in midspring, while it also provides a contrast for richer border colors and the glossy foliage on evergreens. For growing tips, see 'Aladdin' (*page 270*).

PLANT PROFILE	
HEIGHT 14in (35cm)	
SITE Full sun	
SOIL Fertile, free-draining	
HARDINESS Z3–8 H8–1	
FLOWERING Midspring	

OTHER VARIETY *T.* 'Galata' (orange-red with yellow at the base).

T

Tulipa 'Queen of Night' Tulip

FROM A DISTANCE, *Tulipa* 'Queen of Night' looks like it is black, but get up close and it is really deep maroon. Highly rated because it is such an unusual color for any spring flower, let alone a tulip, it makes a strong contrast with whites and yellows. By itself it can look a bit maudlin, but in the right color scheme it is a definite hit. For growing tips, see 'Aladdin' (*page 270*).

OTHER VARIETY *T.* 'Union Jack' (contrasting ivory white with raspberry red markings).

PLANT PROFILE

HEIGHT 24in (60cm)

SITE Full sun

SOIL Fertile, free-draining

HARDINESS Z3–8 H8–1

FLOWERING Late spring

Tulipa 'Red Riding Hood' Tulip

T

A HIGHLY APPROPRIATE NAME for the tomato red flowers that
are scarlet on the inside, with a black base. The leaves are nicely
colored with dark blue-maroon marks. Its short height means
that *Tulipa* 'Red Riding Hood' is ideal for rock gardens, gaps along
the patio, or a position toward the front of a border, and it is a sharp
attention-grabber when the sun is out. See 'Aladdin' (*page 270*)
for growing tips.

PLANT PROFILE	
HEIGHT 8in (20cm)	
SITE Full sun	
SOIL Fertile, free-draining	
HARDINESS Z3–8 H8–1	
FLOWERING Early spring	

OTHER VARIETY *T.* 'Toronto' (salmon orange flowers).

T | *Tulipa saxatilis* Cretan tulip

THE PINK TO LILAC PURPLE FLOWERS of *Tulipa saxatilis* have white margins with yellow marks, and there is a green flush to the outer petals. The leaves are distinctive, being rich green with a red edge, and appear at the start of winter, well before the flowers. In the wild it grows in Crete, where it gets a summer baking, which is also just what it needs in gardens. It can be left outside all year if it gets a free-draining hot spot—for example, at the foot of a sunny wall; otherwise, see 'Aladdin' (*page 270*) for growing tips.

OTHER VARIETY *T. saxatilis* Bakeri Group (bell-shaped, mauve-purple flowers).

PLANT PROFILE
HEIGHT 14in (35cm)
SITE Full sun
SOIL Fertile, free-draining
HARDINESS Z3–8 H8–1
FLOWERING Mid- and late spring

Tulipa 'Schoonoord' Tulip

T

THE LARGE, WHITE, DOUBLE FLOWERS of *Tulipa* 'Schoonoord' are highly rated by the experts, and make a nice contrast with any of the blue-flowered spring bulbs, or among the richer-colored tulips. It can be grown in front of hedges or shrubs with glossy, evergreen leaves, and looks highly effective framing a piece of topiary, but is equally at home in formal and cottage gardens. For growing tips, see 'Aladdin' (*page 270*).

PLANT PROFILE	
HEIGHT 12in (30cm)	
SITE Full sun	
SOIL Fertile, free-draining	
HARDINESS Z3–8 H8–1	
FLOWERING Midspring	

OTHER VARIETY *T.* 'Boule de Neige' (pure white flowers).

T | *Tulipa sprengeri* Tulip

IF YOU WANT TO STRETCH THE TULIP SEASON up to the start of summer, *Tulipa sprengeri* is a good choice because it is one of the last to flower. Other attractions are the flashy red to orange-red blooms, and the fact it also tolerates light shade in borders and short grass, where it can be left outside all year. *T. sprengeri* is excellent when scattered under a white-flowered magnolia. See 'Aladdin' (*page 270*) for growing tips.

OTHER VARIETY *T.* 'Blue Heron' (purple-fringed, violet purple flowers).

PLANT PROFILE

HEIGHT 20in (50cm)

SITE Full sun to light shade

SOIL Fertile, free-draining

HARDINESS Z3–8 H8–1

FLOWERING Early summer

Tulipa 'Spring Green' Tulip

T

THE CREAMY, NOT-QUITE-WHITE *Tulipa* 'Spring Green' has a green stripe of feathering on each petal, both inside and out. It belongs to the Viridiflora Group, which provides very good cut flowers. In the garden it is worth growing in an elegant area because it has a certain degree of style, but it is by no means out of place in a cottage garden. See 'Aladdin' (*page 270*) for growing tips.

PLANT PROFILE	
HEIGHT 16in (40cm)	
SITE Full sun	
SOIL Fertile, free-draining	
HARDINESS Z3–8 H8–1	
FLOWERING Late spring	

OTHER VARIETY *T.* 'Groenland' (green with rose pink margins).

T

Tulipa sylvestris Wild tulip

A WILD TULIP WITH A FAINT SCENT, *T. sylvestris* is usually a golden color, flushed with green on the outside; occasionally the flowers are cream. It can be grown in short grass as well as in borders, but the flowering will be more limited. *T. sylvestris* has a reputation for being easily grown, and was once even regarded as a weed, but the lack of flowers will deter all but the committed tulipophile. Given free-draining soil, it can be left outside all year; otherwise, see 'Aladdin' (*page 270*) for growing tips.

PLANT PROFILE
HEIGHT 18in (45cm)
SITE Full sun to light shade
SOIL Fertile, free-draining
HARDINESS Z3–8 H8–1
FLOWERING Mid- and late spring

Tulipa turkestanica Tulip

T

THE CREAMY WHITE FLOWERS of *Tulipa turkestanica* have a green-gray or green-pink flush on the outside. There is also a dash of orange in the center of the petals. The flowers are faintly but rather unpleasantly scented, though you have to get up extremely close to notice. *T. turkestanica* can be grown in rock or gravel gardens, where it can be left outside all year given free-draining soil. Otherwise, grow as for 'Aladdin' (*see page 270*).

OTHER VARIETY *T. violacea* (star-shaped violet-purple flowers with yellow or black-blue marks at the bases).

PLANT PROFILE
HEIGHT 12in (30cm)
SITE Full sun
SOIL Fertile, free-draining
HARDINESS Z3–8 H8–1
FLOWERING Early and midspring

T

Tulipa 'West Point' Tulip

THE FLASHY MIX OF BRIGHT YELLOW, star-shaped 'West Point' tulips above a mass of blue forget-me-nots might be the biggest cliché in gardening, with photographs of the combination plastered throughout countless books and magazines, but it is still a thrilling mix and well worth trying. 'West Point' can also be used in a wide range of other settings—the more elegant, the better, given its long, pointed petals. For growing tips, see 'Aladdin' (*page 270*).

OTHER VARIETY *T.* 'Maytime' (red-violet flowers with white-margined, yellow bases).

PLANT PROFILE	
HEIGHT	20in (50cm)
SITE	Full sun
SOIL	Fertile, free-draining
HARDINESS	Z3–8 H8–1
FLOWERING	Late spring

Tulipa 'White Parrot' Tulip

T

A GOOD CHOICE FOR AN INFORMAL or cottage garden because *Tulipa* 'White Parrot' lacks the smart, elegant, shapely style of some tulips and has a distinctly ruffled, frilly look. It is well worth planting when you need a bright combination with red or bluish tulips, or a burst of spring bulbs to go in front of an evergreen hedge or shrub. Use it with the other, often zany, parrot varieties, many of which come in startling colors like the red and yellow 'Flaming Parrot'. See 'Aladdin' (*page 270*) for growing tips.

OTHER VARIETY *T.* 'Estella Rijnveld' (*see page 282*).

PLANT PROFILE
HEIGHT 22in (55cm)
SITE Full sun
SOIL Fertile, free-draining
HARDINESS Z3–8 H8–1
FLOWERING Late spring

V | *Veltheimia bracteata* Forest lily

THE FLOWERS OF *Veltheimia bracteata* look like a cluster of small tubes packed together at the top of the stem. They are pink–purple with yellow spots, and the glossy green leaves are virtually evergreen. Being a tender South African, it is usually grown in pots in a conservatory. Set bulbs in a loam-based potting mix with added horticultural sand to improve drainage, in early autumn. Make sure that the tip of the bulb is visible above the soil. Provide weak tomato fertilizer every two weeks when in full growth. Reduce watering as the leaves start dying down, and keep just moist when dormant. Only repot when the container is packed with roots, because this bulb really hates being disturbed.

PLANT PROFILE

HEIGHT 18in (45cm)

SPREAD 12in (30cm)

SITE Full sun

SOIL Loam-based potting mix

HARDINESS Z13–15 H12–10

FLOWERING Spring

Watsonia pillansii Bugle lily

A COLORFUL ORANGE TO ORANGE-RED South African bulb, *Watsonia pillansii* will probably be too tender for many areas but can easily be grown in conservatory pots. Fill them with loam-based potting mix with added horticultural sand and leaf mold. Water freely when in growth and apply liquid fertilizer every month. When dormant, keep it just moist. If you want to try growing it outside, plant it at the foot of a sheltered, sunny wall where the soil is free-draining. As a precaution, add a protective winter mulch to insulate the roots.

OTHER VARIETY *W. aletroides* (orange-red flowers).

PLANT PROFILE
HEIGHT 20–48in (50–120cm)
SPREAD 4in (10cm)
SITE Full sun
SOIL Light, free-draining, moist in summer
HARDINESS Z11–13 H12–6
FLOWERING Summer to autumn

Z | *Zephyranthes candida* Rainflower

THIS SOUTH AMERICAN BULB is worth growing for two
reasons. First, it has a succession of crocuslike, pure white flowers,
sometimes with a red tint on the back of the petals. Second, it is the
hardiest of the zephyranthes and therefore the easiest one to grow.
It does need a free-draining hot spot, and if it is left in the ground
all year, it might need a protective winter mulch. If you grow it in
conservatory pots, use loam-based potting mix with added
horticultural sand. Water freely when in growth, applying a liquid
fertilizer every four weeks. Keep just moist in winter.

OTHER VARIETY *Z. rosea* (pink flowers).

PLANT PROFILE

HEIGHT 4–8in (10–20cm)

SPREAD 3in (8cm)

SITE Full sun

SOIL Moist but free-draining

HARDINESS Z7–9 H9–6

FLOWERING Early autumn

Zigadenus elegans White camas

Z

A LOVER OF DAMP MEADOWS, and growing the length of North America, *Zigadenus elegans* has spikes of small, star-shaped, green-white flowers above 12in- (30cm-) long, gray-green leaves (*see inset*). It is a useful addition to the mid- and late summer border, but if you can only find *Z. glaucus*, buy that instead, because only botanists are likely to spot the difference. To grow either in conservatory pots, use a loam-based potting mix with added horticultural sand, and plant the bulbs 6–8in (15–20cm) deep. Put them in a frost-free spot over the winter.

OTHER VARIETY *Z. fremontii* (creamy white flowers).

PLANT PROFILE
HEIGHT 28in (70cm)
SPREAD 3in (8cm)
SITE Full sun or partial shade
SOIL Rich, moist but free-draining
HARDINESS Z5–9 H9–5
FLOWERING Mid- and late summer

Bulb suppliers

You should find many of the bulbs in this book at garden centers, but for more unusual varieties, try these specialist suppliers

Bloms Bulbs, Inc.
491-233 Glen Eagle Square
Glen Mills, PA 19342
(866) 7-TULIPS
www.blomsbulbs.com

Blooming Bulb Company
1133 South Riverside #16
Medford, OR 97501
(800) 648-2852
www.bloomingbulb.com

Brent and Becky's Bulbs
7900 Daffodil Lane
Gloucester, VA 23061
(804) 693-3966
www.brentandbeckysbulbs.com

Dutch Gardens
144 Intervale Road
Burlington, VT 05401
(800) 944-2250
www.dutchgardens.com

GardeningBulbs.com
9735A Bethel Road
Frederick, MD 21702
(301) 694-6072
www.gardeningbulbs.com

Geerlings Bulbs USA
P.O. Box 843
Babylon, NY 11702
(703) 783-6237
www.dutchflowers.com

John Scheepers. Inc.
23 Tulip Drive
Bantam, CT 06750
(860) 567-0838
www.johnscheepers.com

Kankakee Valley Flowers
3237 South 8500E Road
Saint Anne, IL
(877) 729-6040
www.kankakeevalleyflowers.com

ngeveld Bulb Company
5 Vassar Avenue
kewood, NJ 08701
32) 367-2000
ww.langeveld.com

ichigan Bulb Company
). Box 4180
wrenceburg, IN 47025-4180
13) 354-1497
ww.michiganbulb.com

cClure & Zimmerman
)8 West Winnebago Street
iesland, WI 53935-0368
00) 883-6998
ww.mzbulb.com

esselaar Bulb Co. Inc.
50 County Road, Route 1A
swich, MA 01938
78) 356-3737
ww.tulipbulbs.com

)ld House Gardens
36 Third Street
nn Arbor, MI 48103
734) 995-1486
ww.oldhousegardens.com

Roozengaarde
15867 Beaver Marsh Road
Mount Vernon, WA 98273
(866) 488-5477
www.tulips.com

Schipper & Company, USA
P.O. Box 7584
Greenwich, CT 06836
(888) 847-8637
www.colorblends.com

Tulip World
P.O. Box 758
Chadds Ford, PA 19317
www.tulipworld.com

Van Bourgondien Brothers
P.O. Box 1000
Babylon, NY 11702
(800) 622-9959
www.dutchbulbs.com

Wooden Shoe Bulb Company
33814 South Meridian Road
Woodburn, OR 97071
(800) 711-2006
www.woodenshoe.com

320 • ACKNOWLEDGMENTS

The publisher would like to thank the following for their kind permission to reproduce their photographs:

Abbreviation key: t=top, b=below, r=right, l=left, c=center, a=above

3: Steven Wooster; **6:** Steve Wooster (br), Steven Wooster (tl); **7:** Steve Wooster (bl), Steven Wooster (cra); **14:** GPL/Chris Burrows; **19:** GPL/Chris Burrows; **20:** Garden World Images; **22:** Roger Smith/DK, Roger Smith/DK (tr); **26:** Clive Nichols; **29:** John Glover; **31:** Roger Smith/DK; **34:** GPL/Rex Butcher; **35:** Garden World Images (t); **44:** Garden World Images; **49:** Photos Horticultural; **52:** Eric Crichton Photos; **53:** A-Z Botanical Collection/Adrian Thomas; **59:** Roger Smith/DK; **60:** Photos Horticultural; **66:** Clive Nichols; **81:** Roger Smith/DK; **86:** Roger Smith/DK; **87:** Roger Smith/DK; **88:** Aylett Nurseries; **90:** John Fielding; **94:** Roger Smith/DK; **97:** GPL/Chris Burrows; **99:** Photos Horticultural (cr); **100:** Roger Smith/DK; **103:** Roger Smith/DK; **106:** Andrew Lawson; **108:** bloompictures/Adrian Bloom; **109:** Roger Smith/DK; **110:** Photos Horticultural; **113:** Garden and Wildlife Matters; **114:** Photos Horticultural; **115:** Garden World Images; **121:** Roger Smith/DK, Roger Smith/DK (tr); **129:** A-Z Botanical Collection/Mike Danson; **132:** bloompictures/Adrian Bloom; **133:** Andrew Lawson (tr), Garden World Images; **136:** Garden World Images; **138:** Garden World Images; **141:** Photos Horticultural; **144:** Garden World Images; **147:** John Glover; **148:** Roger Smith/DK; **149:** Roger Smith/DK (tr); **151:** GPL/Howard Rice, Garden World Images (tr); **154:** Photos Horticultural; **156:** Photos Horticultural; **158:** Botanical Collection/Adrian Thomas; **159:** A-Z Botanical Collection/Helmut Partsch; **160:** Ro Smith/DK; **161:** Garden World Images; **164:** Garden World Images; **166:** Roger Smith/DK; **171:** Roger Smith/DK; **176:** Roge Smith/DK; **186:** Andrew Lawson, Garden Worl Images (cr); **187:** Roger Smith/DK; **188:** Roge Smith/DK; **189:** Garden World Images; **190:** Roger Smith/DK; **191:** Garden World Images; **196:** Andrew Butler; **197:** Roger Smith/DK (tr); **206:** Roger Smith/DK; **217:** Roger Smith/DK, Roger Smith/DK (cr); **219:** Roger Smith/DK; **226:** Roger Smith/DK **240:** Roger Smith/DK; **241:** Roger Smith/DK **244:** Jonathan Buckley; **245:** Clive Nichols; **247:** Beth Chatto; **248:** A-Z Botanical Collection/Malkolm Warrington; **249:** A-Z Botanical Collection/Alan Gould; **250:** A-Z Botanical Collection/Ron Bass; **251:** Clive Nichols; **253:** Garden World Images, Garden World Images (tr); **257:** Andrew Lawson; **262:** A-Z Botanical Collection/Irene Windridge **282:** Roger Smith/DK (tr); **283:** Garden World Images; **287:** A-Z Botanical Collection/Adrian Thomas (tr), Photos Horticultural; **290:** John Glover; **291:** Photos Horticultural; **292:** Photos Horticultural; **295:** Roger Smith/DK; **300:** Rog Smith/DK; **301:** Photos Horticultural, Roger Smith/DK (cr); **312:** Eric Crichton Photos; **314:** Photos Horticultural; **315:** Garden World Images, Garden World Images (tr).

All other images © Dorling Kindersley.
For further information, see www.dkimages.com